TYRANNY 2.0

TYRANNY 2.0

SATAN'S WAR OF TERROR

SAID MIRZA

Men of God Publishing

The Qur'an: A Complete Revelation © Sam Gerrans, 2021.
The Meaning of the Holy Qur'an © Abdullah Yusuf Ali, 1938.
The Holy Bible, King James Version.

First Edition, 2021

ISBN 978-1-7336408-3-1

Men of God Publishing
www.willyounotreason.com

And We have made the Qur'an easy to remember, so
  is there any who will remember?
And the warnings came to the people of Pharaoh.
They denied all of Our signs, so We seized them with
  the seizing of One Exalted in Might, Omnipotent.
Are your rejecters better than those? Or have you
  immunity in the writings?
(The Qur'an, 54:40-43)

CONTENTS

ACKNOWLEDGMENTS

I am indebted to God the Almighty for guiding me to His light when I was stumbling in the depths of darkness. It is His bestowal of grace, favor and strength that has allowed me to undertake this arduous task of speaking the truth and warning men. All good in it is from God alone and all errors are mine alone.

I wish to thank my family for their unwavering support and commitment to my mission.

I wish to thank my friend and brother in faith, Sam Gerrans, for his help, support and advice in every step of my task. I have learned a lot from him over the years.

I wish to thank Amatullah Bantley, Edward W. Lane, Emily Assami, Hans Bodo Gerhardt Wehr, Kais Dukes, J.G. Hava, J. Milton Cowan, John J. Arberry, Mary Kennedy, Muhammad Asad, Muhammad Marmaduke Pickthall, and Stanley Lane-Poole; I have benefited immensely from their labors.

Finally, I am grateful to the late Alan Watt for sharing his wealth of knowledge.

May God give them all their just rewards.

INTRODUCTION

We are living in a Satanic tyranny disguised as a democracy. The genius of its architects is that they have camouflaged it in the doublespeak of choice, freedom and democracy; but make no mistake, we face a tyranny unparalleled by any of its predecessors in its scale and sophistication. Whereas, the tyrannies of old employed crude methods of torture and mass slaughter to subjugate the masses; Tyranny 2.0 employs the refined scientific method. It applies knowledge gained from the disciplines of biology, chemistry, computer science, mathematics, physics and psychology in its management of the human herd; continuously learning, refining its algorithms and perfecting its methods in order to achieve its ultimate goal of complete control over the human mind.

The fake pandemic of 2020 kicked off the global implementation of totalitarian lockdowns, mandatory face masks and forced injections. This is but a taste of the dystopian future that awaits us if we do not repent, reform and warn. It may sound cliché, but time *is* running out. Tyranny 2.0 is now officially online and our technocratic overlords have made it clear that they mean business.

Yet, even now, most men are unaware (or in denial) that we are living under a tyranny. The truth is that "God guides whom He wills".[1] It is not within my power to *wake* you up, nor can I convince a victim of brainwashing that he, in fact, *is* brainwashed. This book is only for those who understand that we are in the grips of a sophisticated tyranny, and believe in

---

1 *The Qur'an*, 28:56.

God; for it is God alone who can save us.

The harsh reality is that we are ruled by corrupt, sinful and evil men. It makes no difference whether they call themselves Christians, Jews, Muslims or atheists, nor does it matter whether they are the leaders of the "free world", third-world dictators, directors of intelligence agencies or the Pharaohs of Egypt, these men are workers of corruption and have no qualms about ordering the slaughter of millions to get what they want.

Contrary to popular propaganda, the rulers of our current tyranny are not the champions of the people, but are their very enemies. This is to be expected since the corrupt selection process of Tyranny 2.0 ensures that only the most vile and devious of the lot rise to the top of the power structure.

These evildoers – and their predecessors – have been waging a secret war against mankind for the better part of a century. Their aim is to destroy our dignity, decency and morality. Ultimately, they wish to extinguish our very soul.

Tyranny 2.0 uses cutting edge *soft* weapons against its principal enemy: men. It uses cellphones, email and social media to track, monitor and surveil us. It leverages the internet and television to deliver devastating payloads of propaganda, pornography and entertainment to keep us docile and apathetic. It markets pharmaceutical weapons of pills, injections and packaged foods to deliver toxic chemicals that destroy our health. It funds social movements to promote homosexuality, women liberation and racial equality to pervert our culture. When all else fails, it deploys drones, smart bombs and mercenaries to kill, slaughter and torture, to obliterate entire nations.

Any reasonable thinking man can now work out that the motive behind such monstrous acts is not "to champion liberty and democracy"[2] across the world. We have been conditioned to accept such outright lies by those in power because this entire system is based on deception.

Tyrants wage war in order to control systems, resources, and

2 Biden, Joseph R., and Jr. "Why America Must Lead Again." Foreign Affairs, Council on Foreign Relations, 30 Nov. 2020, www.foreignaffairs.com/articles/united-states/2020-01-23/why-america-must-lead-again.

people. They know that they must control all resources in order to guarantee their position as the apex predator. However, our enlightened tyrants have come to understand that if they wish to rule forever, they must ultimately control the human mind; and they are tantalizingly close to their goal.

The first rule of any conflict is to know your enemy. All evidence implicates the United States – considering its superpower status – as the primary cultural, economic and environmental corrupter in the land, but that is seeing the trees for the forest. The people of the United States – and the Western civilization – have, themselves, been under a continuous assault by a sinister force for the better part of a century. It was only after this force of evil had compromised the religion, culture and family values of the West that it set its sights upon the rest of the world.

What is this sinister force and why is it hell bent on destroying humanity? You may already have a hazy idea of its nature even though modern propaganda has done all that it can to convince you of its non-existence. I am, of course, talking about Satan, the Deceiver. Tyranny 2.0 is based entirely on deception precisely because it is a Satanic tyranny and, as we shall see, deception is *the* modus operandi of Satan.

God in His final revelation to mankind, the Qur'an, warns us of this malevolent being whose objective is nothing short of our utter humiliation and destruction. The seriousness of God's warning cannot be overstated. He exhorts us to take Satan as a clear enemy and exercise our utmost vigilance against his attempts to divert us from the righteous path of God. Satan wishes to enslave us in this world and lead us to Hell in the next; and he achieves this by partnering with tyrants, old and new.

The Qur'an details the account of an ancient tyrant, Pharaoh, who, similarly, was in the thrall of Satan. He used religion, sorcery and finance to subjugate its population; not unlike Tyranny 2.0 which uses science, the entertainment industry and banks to subjugate us. Pharaoh's tyranny committed genocide by slaughtering a certain faction of the population; not unlike Tyranny 2.0 which commits global genocide – the depopulation agenda – by the scientific means of feeding the populace processed GMO foods and pesticide tainted crops, facilitating abortion and, more recently, COVID-19 "vaccines". Pharaoh sought to discover the God of Moses and the means of the heavens; not unlike Tyranny 2.0 which is launching sophisticated telescopes and satellites to peer into the heavens, and constructing state-of-the-art particle accelerators to study the building blocks of the universe.

But, perhaps, the most striking of all connections between Pharaoh's tyranny and Tyranny 2.0 is their use of the obelisk to mark their dominion. These obelisks are now erected in all major cities around the world. The most famous of them, the Washington Monument, is a popular tourist attraction in Washington D.C. Every President of the United States faces this obelisk during his swearing in ceremony, promising to protect and defend Tyranny 2.0.

Satan uses the elites of Tyranny 2.0 to implement his agenda of enslaving mankind; and they are rewarded well for their services. However, theirs is a losing deal because on the Day of Judgment, Satan and his followers will enter Hell and remain there forever; an evil end for evil works. If that was the end of the matter, I would not be writing this book. But, unfortunately, it is not.

The people – by informed consent and active participation in this Satanic system – are guilty as well. They worship the idols of Tyranny 2.0 instead of worshipping God. They turn to the idols of state, religion and medicine to seek safety, guidance and health, when they should be seeking these blessings from God. They worship themselves when they should be worshipping God. They fear men when they should be fearing God. These tendencies are termed as *making partners with God* within the theology of the Qur'an, the only unforgivable sin.[3] If the people do not repent and reform, they will enter Hell along with their leaders.

This is a spiritual war and at stake is our very soul. The pain, suffering and humiliation that we experience in this life is but a shadow of the eternal pain and suffering that awaits

---

3 *The Qur'an* 4:48.

the apathetic, amoral, and appetite driven souls in Hell, unless they repent and reform.

The Qur'an calls those who believe in God and the life to come to work on disciplining and purifying themselves. They must stop consuming the filth churned out by Tyranny 2.0 and struggle to escape, as much as possible, from its grip. God promises His help, provision and refuge to those who resist Satan and assures them a place in the eternal Garden in the Hereafter. We must warn men of the impending judgment of God which will can only be averted from those who fear God and take the Almighty as their sole Ally and Protector.

***

Many of the ideas presented in this book are from the ground-breaking work of Sam Gerrans titled *The Qur'an: A Complete Revelation*. I encourage you to download his work — which is available for free[4] — and go through it carefully.

I would be remiss if I did not mention the impact Alan Watt's talks[5] — have had on my world-view. His piercing insights into the inner workings of this Satanic system and the staggering scale of its deception have influenced many of my own ideas in this work.

All translations, unless otherwise noted, are my own. I have striven to render the Arabic in a literal, direct and consistent manner, being particularly influenced by the unique styles of John J. Arberry, Sahih International and Sam Gerrans. Where a literal translation of a phrase was too confusing, I have opted for a somewhat looser rendering, but have footnoted the literal translation for the interested reader.

Let us begin then; in the name of God.

---

4 https://quranite.com
5 http://cuttingthroughthematrix.com

1

THE QUR'AN

It is clear to any thinking man that we are living in unprecedented times. The level of duplicity, corruption and apathy is staggering. Under the guise of a fake pandemic, the elites have brought in a totalitarian regime. Almost overnight, like clockwork, the whole world went into lockdown. Mandatory face masks and coerced vaccinations soon followed. Men are being denied the basic right to earn a living to feed their families, causing untold suffering and suicides. The next line item in this agenda, vaccine passports, will usher in pervasive surveillance beyond anything dreamed up by Orwell.

The resistance claims that if enough people wake up, things will change. That is a fallacy.[6] The majority of people are lazy, addicted and selfish. They are unwilling to bear the hardship and loss which invariably comes with standing up for a cause. It is only the few, the believers, who will resist because they understand this to be a spiritual war, the ramifications of which extend beyond this life. God, our Ally, promises us victory if we reform ourselves and deliver God's warning to mankind. We will be tested by God, but if we stand firm, we are assured Paradise, the greatest achievement of all.

---

6 I thank Sam Gerrans for this insight.

Fear of God

If We had sent down this Qur'an upon a mountain,
you would have seen it humbled, split asunder from
fear of God. And those examples – We strike them
for men that they may give thought.
(59:21)

The fear of the LORD *is* the beginning of wisdom:
and the knowledge of the holy *is* understanding.
(Proverbs 9:10)

There is a reason for the spiritual and moral decline of our civilization. Not long ago, men considered promiscuity, deception and exploitation as immoral. Whether they were religious or not, men had an intuitive understanding of moral boundaries – limits set by God – which could not be crossed. They had a fixed idea about good and evil. That was then.

Now, we live in a society that practices moral relativism. Good and evil are relative terms; they depend upon context. This has resulted in the disintegration of all moral absolutes. Pursuit of pleasure is now man's main preoccupation. Immorality and degeneracy are now celebrated by society. Science, the great religion of our day, has altogether dispensed with God. It postulates that since no God exists, there is no need to fear Him. The only thing to be feared is the state. This, of course, is a prerequisite for all tyrannies, because as long as a man fears God, he will not submit to a tyranny.

Decadence is the hallmark of every failed civilization. Satan's first attack on Adam's God-given dignity was to reveal his shame to him by removing his clothes. He continues his attack on the dignity of Adam's progeny by whispering sexual immorality, depravity and perversion to them. This is why Tyranny 2.0 actively promotes pornography, fornication and homosexuality, for it is only when man sinks to the level of a beast, that Satan can subject him to his tyranny; the stronger man's enslavement to his base desires, the stronger the shackles of Satan's tyranny.

God's mercy

But, not all hope is lost. God, in His mercy, has sent down the Qur'an, a beacon guiding to the most upright behavior. He offers man a chance to reclaim his lost noble station, if he turns to God, repents and follows His guidance; the Qur'an. God calls us to trust in Him and abandon all false gods. It is only by submitting to God completely, working righteousness and warning men of the Day of Judgment that we have any hope of resisting this tyranny and avoiding Hell.

> A revelation from the Almighty, the Merciful.
> A Book whose signs have been detailed as an Arabic
>   recitation for a people who know,
> A bearer of good news, and a warner, but most of
>   them turn away, so they do not hear.
> (41:2-4)

> Say, "If men and the elites[7] gathered to bring the like
>   of this Qur'an, they could not bring the like of it,
>   even if some of them were helpers to some."
> (17:88)

The average Muslim

Muslims – not unlike the generality of mankind – are unaware of the pressing need to believe, repent and reform. Like the Christians and Jews, they assume that they are already saved; a bold assumption indeed.

The average Muslim believes the Qur'an to be too complicated relying upon his favorite religious scholar[8] to explain it to him. More accurately, he is looking for confirmation that his inherited ideas, rituals and world-view find some purchase in the Qur'an, so he can continue to follow his ancestors blindly. The thought that he may be wrong or that his ancestors might have been misguided does not even cross his mind.

---

7 I give credit to Brother Gerrans for this translation who translates this word as *domini*.

8 *ulema, imam, sheikh, mufti*, etc.

Muslims' engagement with the Qur'an is generally limited to reciting – usually, without any understanding – of select short chapters from the Qur'an during a specific ritual which they conflate with the *al-salaat* in the Qur'an. Muslims think that by reciting the Qur'an in Arabic – whether they understand it or not – they earn rewards, and if they accumulate sufficient rewards, they will enter Paradise.

Conspicuously, the five articles of faith[9] which form the foundation of Islam, nowhere, mention the study of God's Book; a telling omission.

Muslims' ignorance of their foundational scripture is hardly surprising; on the contrary, it is predicted by the Qur'an itself. On the Day of Resurrection, Prophet Muhammad will say:

> And the messenger will say, "O my Lord, my people
> took this Qur'an as absurd."[10]
> (25:30)

Supplanting the Qur'an by means of the hadith

> And fulfilled is the word of your Lord in truthfulness
> and justice; none can change His words; and He is
> the Hearing, the Knowing.
> (6:115)

Since Muslims were unable to change the word of God i.e. the Qur'an to support their religion, they did the next best thing; they altered the meanings of the words in the Qur'an and invented a separate *hadith* literature – sayings attributed to Prophet Muhammad – to explain and expand upon these altered Qur'anic terms. Using this tactic, they were able to supplant the Qur'an using the *hadith* and graft an alien religion onto the Qur'an. This is not anything new as the Jews had done something similar with their revelation, the Torah.

---

9 Also known as the five pillars of Islam.
10 The primary idea is that they treated it as an archaic book, not relevant to their day and age.

> Do you hope that they will believe you? And a faction
> of them had heard God's word, then altered it after
> they had understood it, and they know.
>
> (2:75)

Islamic religious scholars interpret the Qur'an using the *hadith* literature – sayings attributed to Prophet Muhammad – while ignoring the fact that the Qur'an claims to be complete.[11] They insist upon taking both the Qur'an and the *hadith* as the basis for their religion because they cannot find the specifics of their inherited rites and rituals – so central to their religion – in the Qur'an. They do not stop to consider that perhaps the reason for their absence is because they are not part of *the faith*[12] in the Qur'an; they are part of the religion of Islam which is not native to the Qur'an.

The stone idol

It is clear to any man possessing insight that the ritual of *Hajj* – in which Muslims circle the *Kaaba*[13] seven times – is a pagan ritual; at its core Islam reveres this stone idol and commands its followers to prostrate towards it five times a day. Muslims are blindly following the footsteps of their forefathers thinking that they were guided.

> O mankind, eat of what is in the ground allowed and
> good, and do not follow the footsteps of Satan. He
> is a clear enemy to you.
> He only commands you to evil and indecency, and
> that you say about God what you know not.
> And when it is said to them, "Follow what God has
> sent down," they say, "Rather, we will follow that
> which we found our fathers doing." Even though
> their fathers did not understand anything, nor were
> they guided?
>
> (2:168-170)

---

11 See 6:115, 14:52, 17:12.

12 Arabic: *al-din*. We shall look at this concept in detail later.

13 A cuboid structure located in Mecca, Saudi Arabia.

Muslims circling and revering the Kaaba

Religion

Religion is the oldest form of control. The elites are the inventors, leaders and supporters of religion using it to subjugate and pacify the masses. The Roman Emperor Constantine I, recognized and formalized Christianity when he convened the first Council of Nicaea in 325 AD. It was only after this watershed event that Christianity really took off.

More recently, the founder of the Saud dynasty, Muhammad bin Saud, backed Muhammad ibn Abd-al-Wahhab, the creator of Wahabbism. Using its revenue from oil exports, the house of Saud exports this extremist sect all over the world, radicalizing men and creating chaos.

In contrast, the prophets and messengers of God came not to bind the masses in the shackles of religion, but to free them from its grip. They called men to the true faith; and were persecuted for it.

And thus We have made for every Prophet an enemy
— adversaries[14] from men and the elites, some of
them inspiring to some, embellished speech in
deceit.[15] And had your Lord willed, they would not
have done it, so leave them and what they invent.
And that the hearts of those who believe not in the
Hereafter may incline to it, and that they may be
pleased with it, and that they may earn what they
are earning.
Is it other than God I should seek as a judge? And it is
He who sent down the Book to you, detailed. And
those to whom We have given the Book know that
it is sent down from your Lord with the truth; so be
not of the doubters.
And completed is the Word of your Lord in truthfulness
and justice. None can change His words, and He is
the Hearing, the Knowing.
(6:112-115)

Muslims are happy blindly emulating the rituals of their
forefathers. The Qur'an, on the other hand, is not concerned
with blind imitation, but with understanding. This discordance
between the Qur'an and Islam is because the religion of Islam
has nothing to do with the Qur'an.[16] On the contrary, it diverts
its followers from the Qur'an. This is not accidental. The religion
of Islam was carefully crafted under the direction of ancient
tyrants who wished to obfuscate its message;[17] a clear and direct
threat to their oppressive system. Islam, like all religions, diverts
men from recognizing their core responsibilities towards their
Creator into performing useless rituals.

However, there are a few who are not satisfied with the
superficialities of religion. They seek to understand the world
and to fathom their true purpose. They wish to worship God
sincerely. The Qur'an addresses such men. It calls them to

---

14 I credit Brother Gerrans for this translated word.
15 In modern parlance, presidents and their speechwriters or fantastic stories
found in *hadith* and similar literature.
16 I credit Brother Gerrans for this point.
17 I credit Brother Gerrans for this point.

repent, believe and reform; to deliver God's messages and actively resist evil. They will be attacked and ridiculed like the men of God – messengers, prophets and believers – before them. However, God gives assurance to them that their actions are not in vain. God gives good news of His mercy and help, in this life and the Hereafter, to those who stand up against tyranny; who fear neither men nor tyrants, but God alone.

The Qur'an is a guidance for mankind

The message of the Qur'an is not limited to a specific tribe, race or culture, but for all mankind. God commands us to completely surrender to Him completely and only seek forgiveness, help, guidance, provision and safety from Him. God commands us to exclusively worship Him and cease the worship of the idols of wealth, power, government, religion, leaders etc. God promises success to those who follow His command and humiliation to those who turn away.

> A moon of *Ramadan*, wherein the Qur'an was sent down, a guidance for mankind and clear signs of guidance and division. So whoso from you witnessed the moon, let him fast in it; and whoso is sick or on a journey, then a number of other days. God intends ease for you and does not intend difficulty for you; and that you complete the number, and magnify God that He has guided you, and that you may be grateful.
>
> (2:185)

> This Qur'an guides to the way that is most upright, and gives good news to the believers who work righteousness that theirs is a great reward.
>
> (17:9)

The Qur'an is a warning

Say, "What thing is greatest in testimony?" Say, "God
is witness between me and you, and this Qur'an
was reveled to me that I may warn you with it, and
whomever it reaches. Do you testify that there are
other gods with God?" Say, "I do not testify." Say,
"He is only One God, and I am free of what you
make partners."
(6:19)

And We have not taught him poetry, nor does is it
behoove him. It is not but a reminder and a clear
Qur'an,
That he may warn whoever is living, and that the
Word[18] may be justified against the rejecters.
(36:69-70)

And thus We have inspired to thee an Arabic
recitation, that you may warn the capital of cities
and those around it, and that you warn of the Day
of Gathering, wherein is no doubt. A faction in
Paradise, and a faction in the Blaze.
(42:7)

The Qur'an is a reminder

And We have contrasted in this Qur'an, that they may
be reminded; and it does not increase them except
in aversion.
(17:41)

We have not sent down the Qur'an upon you that you
be wretched,
But only as a reminder to him who fears,
A revelation from Him who created the land and the
high skies;
(20:2-4)

---

18 See 38:84.

And thus We have sent it down as an Arabic Qur'an,
and We have contrasted in it of the Threat, that
they may be godfearing, or it may relate to them a
reminder.

(20:113)

Sad. By the Qur'an possessing a reminder.

(38:1)

We are most knowing of what they say, and you are
not a compeller over them. So remind by the Qur'an
him who fears My threat.

(50:45)

And We have made the Qur'an easy for remembrance,
so is there any who will remember?

(54:17)

The Qur'an requires contemplation

We sent it down as an Arabic recitation that you might
understand.

(12:2)

We made it an Arabic recitation that you might
understand.

(43:3)

Do they not ponder the Qur'an, or are there locks
upon their hearts?

(47:24)

The Qur'an negates the Arabs' claim that because it is in
their language it can only be understood by them. The truth
is that God gives understanding of His message to whom He
wills.

10

And if We had made it a recitation in a foreign
  language, they would have said, "Why are its signs
  not detailed? What, a foreign language and an
  Arab?" Say, "It is, for those who believe, a guidance
  and a healing; but those who do not believe, in their
  ears is deafness, and to them it is a blindness; those
  – they are called from a far place."
(41:44)

Every example presented in the Qur'an

And We have contrasted for mankind in this Qur'an of
  every example, but most of mankind refuse except
  rejection.
(17:89)

And We have presented for mankind in this Qur'an
  from every example; and if you bring them a sign,
  those who reject will surely say, "You are but
  falsifiers."
(30:58)

And We have presented for mankind in this Qur'an
  from every example; that they might remember.
An Arabic Qur'an, possessing no deviation; that they
  may be godfearing.
(39:27-28)

The Qur'an is a mercy for the believers

God sent down the Qur'an as a mercy for the believers. Being
a believer has nothing to do with subscribing to a religion; God
gives us the criteria for *believers in truth*.[19]

- They are fearful when God is remembered
- They increase in faith when God's signs are recited to them
- They place their trust in their Lord

---

19 I thank and credit Brother Gerrans for this insight.

- They set upright the duty[20]
- They spend out of what God has provided them[21]
- They believe
- They emigrate
- They strive in God's cause
- They shelter and help other believers[22]

> And We send down of the Qur'an that which is a
> healing and a mercy to the believers; and it increases
> not the oppressors, except in loss.
>
> (17:82)

> *Ta Sin*. Those are the signs of the Qur'an and a clear
> book,
> A Guidance and good news for the believers
> Who set upright the duty, and give the purity, and of
> the Hereafter are certain.
>
> (27:1-3)

---

20 For an excellent analysis of this term, I refer the interested reader to Brother
Gerrans' work: *The Qur'an: A Complete Revelation.*
21 See 8:1-8:4.
22 See 8:74.

2

SATAN

Satan is the title of *Iblees*, a malevolent being created from fire. Satan means *adversary*.[23] In the Qur'an, God repeatedly warns us not to take our adversary, Satan, lightly.

> And We have created man of dry clay from molded
>   sludge.
> And the *al-jann*,[24] We created him before from
>   scorching fire.
>
> (15:26-27)

Iblees – a being created from fire – thinks himself to be superior to man. When God commanded *Iblees* to submit to Adam, he refused. Consequently, God cursed and expelled him from the Heavenly Assembly. However, *Iblees* requested a respite from God to corrupt man; to show Him that man was unworthy of the honor God bestowed upon him. God granted him his request until the Day of Judgment.

Iblees is given the power to whisper to man and tempt him towards evil. His sole objective is to divert man from the straight path of God and lead him into Hell. He uses various tactics, chief among them deception, to mislead man.

We shall look at *Iblees'* tactics in detail later, but first we

---

23 I give credit to Brother Gerrans for this translation.
24 For an excellent analysis of this subject, I refer the interested reader to Brother Gerrans' work: *The Qur'an: A Complete Revelation.*

need to consider Adam's backstory so we can better understand *Iblees'* motivation for despising him and his progeny.

Adam created with a purpose

> Blessed is He in whose hand is the Dominion – He is
> over all things powerful –
> Who created death and life, that He might test you
> which of you is best in works; and He is the Mighty,
> the Forgiving –
>
> (67:1-2)

After creating Adam, God commanded the *malaikah*, the angels, to submit to him. The Arabic word *malaikah* is derived from the root[25] *m-l-k* which means *having possession and command* or *authority.*[26] When God proclaimed that he was making man a successor[27] in the land, it implied a change in ownership of the land, from the angels to man; to which they protested. However, when God commanded them to submit to Adam, they immediately complied, relinquishing their authority to man, except *Iblees.*

> And when your Lord said to the angels, "I am making
> a successor in the land." They said, "Will You place
> therein one will do corruption there, and shed
> blood, while we give glory with Your praise and
> hallow You?" He said, "I know what you do not
> know."
>
> (2:30)

> When you Lord said to the angels, "I am creating a
> human from mud.

---

25 Most Arabic words are derived from a three letter pattern – called a root – that has a specific meaning.
26 Edward William Lane, An Arabic-English Lexicon, ٢٠٢١) ملك. (م,). Retrieved 20 February 2021, from http://www.perseus.tufts.edu/hopper/text?doc=mlk&fromdoc=Perseus:text:2002.02.0046
27 See 2:30.

So when I have fashioned him, and blown My *ruh* in
him, fall to him submitting!"
(38:71-72)

And when your Lord said to the angels, "I am creating
a human of dry clay from molded sludge.
So when I have fashioned him, and blown My *ruh* in
him, fall to him submitting!"
(15:28-29)

God gave Adam the knowledge of all things

God fashioned Adam and blew His *ruh* into him, through
which, He taught him the names of all things. [28]

And He taught Adam the names – all of them. Then He
presented them[29] unto the angels and said, "Inform
Me of the names of these, if you are truthful."
They said, "Glory be to You! No knowledge have we
save what You taught us. You are the Knowing, the
Wise."
He said, "O Adam, inform them of their names." And
when he had informed them of their names, He
said, "Did I not tell you that I know the unseen of
the skies and the land? And I know what you make
evident, and what you were hiding."
(2:31-33)

When God proclaimed that he was creating man, the angels
protested; they feared that man's base nature would lead him
to cause corruption in the land and shed blood.[30] However,
they failed to see the potential within man; he could surpass
them in his fear of God if he had knowledge of God's attributes
and was determined to become righteous.

It is only when man understands the attributes of God

---

28 Throughout history, God's prophets have received revelation from God
through this same *ruh*. See 40:15, 42:52.
29 The phenomena, the names of which God had taught Adam.
30 See 2:30.

Almighty and his relationship and responsibility to Him that he can attain *taqwa* – fear of God – and yearn to please His Lord. Therein lies man's superiority over the angels. The angels can only obey God's commands – or disobey them, in the case of *Iblees* – but man can go a step further; he can make moral decisions based on God given knowledge, thereby pleasing God; or he can make immoral decisions based on his vain desires, thereby displeasing God.

> And God presents an example: two men, one of them dumb, he has no power over anything, and he is a burden upon his master – wherever he directs him, he brings no good. Is he equal to him who commands justice, and is on a straight path?
> (16:76)

Iblees refuses to submit to Adam

> And when We said to the angels, "Submit to Adam", so they submitted, except *Iblees*. He refused, and was arrogant, and he was of the rejecters.
> (2:34)

> And when We said the angels, "Submit to Adam"; so they submitted, except *Iblees;* he was one of the elites,[31] and he rebelled against his Lord's command. Do you then take him and his progeny as allies, other than Me, when they are enemies to you? Wretched is the exchange for the wrongdoers.
> (18:50)

> And when We said to the angels, "Submit to Adam"; so they submitted, except *Iblees*; he refused.
> (20:116)

---

31 I am thankful to Brother Gerrans for the meaning of this word; he translates it as *dominus.* The idea is that *Iblees* was a leader.

Then the angels submitted themselves all together,
Except *Iblees*; he refused to be with those submitting.
(15:30-31)

Then the angels submitted themselves all together,
Except *Iblees*; he was arrogant, and was one of the
    rejecters.
(38:73-74)

Arrogance was *Iblees'* chief sin. Similarly, the arrogant turn away from God's guidance and from worshipping Him.

To Him belongs whoever is in the skies and the land.
    And those near Him are not too arrogant to worship
    Him, nor do they tire,
Glorifying Him night and day, never slackening.
(21:19-20)

I shall turn from My signs those who are arrogant in
    the land without right; though they see every sign,
    they will not believe in it, and though they see the
    way of righteousness, they will not take it for a way,
    and though they see the way of error, they will take
    it for a way. That is because they have denied our
    signs and were heedless.
(7:146)

Iblees allowed to whisper to man

Iblees wrongfully accused God for leading him astray and challenged Him that if he be given respite, he would misguide most men. God granted him respite, allowing him to whisper in the hearts of men; impelling them to corrupt and oppress. All those who follow him will enter Hell.

And *Iblees* confirmed his opinion of them, and they
    followed him, except a faction of the believers.

And he had no authority over them, but that We might
  know him who believes in the Hereafter from him
  who is in uncertainty thereof. And Your Lord, over
  everything, is Guardian.

(34:20-21)

Said he, "Because You led me astray, I shall sit in
  ambush for them on Your straight path;
Then I shall come on them from between their hands,
  and from their behind, and from their right hands
  and their left hands. And You will not find most of
  them grateful."

(7:16-17)

On the Day of Judgment, the respite given to *Iblees* will
expire and all men will be presented to God for judgment. God
has allowed *Iblees* to tempt man so that He may know which of
them *actually* believe in the life to come.

In that are signs, and We are testing.

(23:30)

And We created you, then We formed you, then
  We said to the angels, "Submit to Adam"; so they
  submitted themselves, except *Iblees* – he was not
  of those submitting.
Said He, "What stopped you that you did not submit
  yourself, when I commanded you?" Said he, "I am
  better than he; You created me of fire, and You
  created him of mud."
Said He, "Get you down out of it; it is not for you to
  be arrogant here. So go you forth, you are of the
  debased."

(7:11-13)

Said He, "O *Iblees*, what is the matter with you that
  you are not with the submitting?"

Said he, "I would never submit myself to a human
    whom You created of dry clay from molded sludge."
Said He, "Then go forth from here, you are an outcast.
And upon you is the curse, until the Day of the faith."[32]
    (15:32-35)

Said He, "O *Iblees*, what stopped you from submitting
    yourself to what I created with My hands? Are you
    arrogant, or are you of the exalted ones?"
Said he, "I am better than he; You created me of fire,
    and You created him of mud."
Said He, "So go you forth from here, you are an
    outcast.
And upon you is My curse, until the Day of the faith."
    (38:75-78)

The forbidden tree

After expelling *Iblees*, God commanded Adam and his wife to
inhabit the Garden, warning them of their new adversary. God
allowed them to eat from wherever they wished, but forbade
them from going near a specific tree. Adam and his wife, as we
shall see, failed to take heed.

The Bible claims that this forbidden tree was the tree of
knowledge of good and evil and the reason Adam and his wife
ate from it was because they desired to be wise.[33] I disagree
because God had already taught Adam the *names of all things*
i.e. Adam already *had* knowledge of good and evil.

The fact of the matter is that the tree was evil and Adam
became a wrongdoer by eating from it. The tree was a trial[34] – a
test for Adam and his wife – and represented the limit of God
beyond which Adam was to not transgress.

And We said, "O Adam, reside you, and your wife,
    in Paradise, and eat thereof freely wherever you

---

32 Arabic: *al-din* which literally means recompense; definition found at 82:17-
19.
33 See Genesis. 2:17, Genesis 3:6.
34 A trial, in Qur'anic terms, is a severe test, failing which leads to disbelief.

will; but do not go near this tree, lest you be of the
wrongdoers."
(2:35)

"And O Adam, reside you, and your wife, in Paradise,
and eat thereof freely wherever you will; but do not
go near this tree, lest you be among the wrongdoers."
(7:19)

The lote tree as a trial for mankind

The theme of a trial is also present in the vision of the *ruh*
shown to Muhammad and the mention of an accursed tree in
the Qur'an. Both instances are referred to as "being trials for
mankind".[35]

And when We said to you, "Your Lord has
encompassed[36] mankind," and We did not make the
dream which We showed you and the accursed tree
in the Qur'an, except as a trial for mankind. And We
frighten them, but it increases them not except in
great transgression.
(17:60)

The Qur'an elaborates on this dream shown to Muhammad
in two other places.

By the star when it fell,
Your companion has neither erred, nor strayed,
Nor does he utter from desire.
It is not but an inspiration inspired,
Taught to him by one mighty in power,
Possessor of firmness; he rose,
When he was on the highest horizon.
Then he approached and descended,
And was at a distance of two bows' length, or nearer,
Then He inspired unto His servant what He inspired.

35 See 17:60.
36 To surround, grasp completely, understand fully.

The heart did not lie about what it saw.
So will you dispute with him over what he sees?
And he has seen him in another descent
Near the lote tree[37] of the destination – [38]
Near which is the Garden of habitation –
When there covered the lote tree that which covered;
The vision did not swerve, nor did it transgress.
He has seen from the signs of his Lord, the greatest.
(53:1-18)

No! I swear by the retreaters,
The runners, the sweepers,
And the night when it darkens,
And the dawn when it breathes,
It is the word of a noble messenger
Possessing power, near the Owner of the Throne
  secure,
Obeyed, moreover trustworthy.
Your companion is not possessed;
He saw him on the clear horizon;
He is not of the unseen, withholding.
And it is not the word of an accursed Satan;
So where are you going?
It is not but a reminder to all beings,
For whoever of you wills to be upright;
But you will not, unless God wills, the Lord of all
  Being.
(81:15-29)

We can infer that in his dream, Muhammad saw the *ruh* through which God taught him the Qur'an; the same *ruh* through which God taught the *names of all things* to Adam.

Muhammad's vision of the *ruh* is a trial for mankind because those who reject the fact that God revealed the Qur'an to Muhammad through the *ruh* in effect reject the divine authorship of the Qur'an and the Hereafter. We also

37 A tree with thorns; see 56:28; associated with Christ's thorn jujube.
38 See 19:68-72. "A place to which a person or thing comes at last", excerpt from Lane, Edward William. Arabic-English Lexicon. Islamic Texts Society, 1984.

see an oblique mention of the lote tree in the dream shown to Muhammad.

> Near the lote tree of the destination –
> Near which is the Garden of habitation –
> When there covered the lote tree that which covered;
> The vision did not swerve, nor did it transgress.
> He has seen from the signs of his Lord, the greatest.
> (53:14-18)

We shall now investigate the nature of this lote tree. The Qur'an describes it as a thorny tree[39] and uses it as an example of bad vegetation that sprung up after God's punishment.[40] This coupled with the fact that signs in the Qur'an are primarily used to frighten men[41] leaves only one possibility as to why Muhammad's "vision did not swerve, nor did it transgress" when he saw the lote tree; he was terror-stricken i.e. the lote tree is a warning to mankind and it should frighten them. We find confirmation of this idea in the verse just before the mention of Muhammad's vision and the lote tree.

> And nothing stopped Us from sending the signs except that the formers denied them and We brought *Thamud* the she-camel as a visible sign, but they wronged her. And We do not send the signs, except to frighten.
> And when We said to you, "Your Lord has encompassed[42] mankind," and We did not make the dream which we showed you and the accursed tree in the Qur'an, except as a trial for mankind. And We frighten them, but it increases them not except in great transgression.
> (17:59-60)

The Qur'an also refers to the accursed lote tree as the tree of

---

39 See 56:28.
40 God flooded the region occupied by the people of Sheba. See 34:15-16.
41 See 17:59.
42 To surround, grasp completely, understand fully.

zaqqum. In the Hereafter, those among mankind who denied the Hereafter – and by extension, the existence of this lote tree – will eat from it. A most ironic punishment.

> Is that[43] a better descent, or the tree of *zaqqum*?
> We made it a trial for the wrongdoers.
> It is a tree that emerges from the root of Hell;
> Its branches[44] like the heads of Satans,
> And they eat from it, and fill their bellies from it,
> Then on top of it they have a mixture of boiling water,
> Then their return is to Hell.
> (37:62-68)

> The tree of *zaqqum*.
> Is the food of the sinner,
> Like oil, boiling in the bellies
> Like boiling liquid.
> (44:43-46)

Similarly, in the Hereafter, those who deny the existence of Hell will "eat" from it.

> The Day they will be tried by the Fire,
> "Taste your trial. This is what you were seeking to hasten!"
> (51:13-14)

The forbidden tree as a trial for Adam

We thus arrive at a startling realization about the nature of the tree from which Adam and his wife ate. God had forbidden Adam and his wife from going near this tree because it was *the* tree of *zaqqum*; which is food for the sinner.[45] Adam and his wife became sinners after eating from the tree of *zaqqum*, and cried out to God that they had wronged their souls.

---

43 i.e. Paradise
44 Spathes, appearance
45 See 44:44.

They said, "Our Lord, we have wronged our souls.
And if You do not forgive us, and have mercy upon
us, we will be of the losers."
(7:23)

God wants the best for man, Satan the worst. Satan wanted
to remove the godfearing robes of Adam and his wife in order
to debase them. Pretending to be their sincere advisor, he
played on their fear and greed promising them security and
immortality. However, when Adam and his wife obeyed him
and ate from the tree of *zaqqum*, the opposite happened;
they lost their dominion and were exiled to an earthly mortal
existence. That is because Satan was and is a Deceiver.[46]

So he directed them by deception; and when they
tasted of the tree, their bodies became evident to
them, so they started stitching upon themselves
leaves of Paradise. And their Lord called to them,
"Did I not forbid you from that tree, and say to you,
'Satan is to you a clear enemy'?"
(7:22)

So We said, "O Adam, this is an enemy to you and your
wife. So let him not bring you out from Paradise, so
that you are wretched.
It is neither for you to hunger therein, nor to go naked,
And neither for you to thirst therein, nor to suffer the
sun."
Then Satan whispered[47] to him; he said, "O Adam,
shall I direct you to the tree of eternity, and a
dominion that does not deteriorate?"
So they both ate of it, and their bodies became evident
to them, and they started stitching upon themselves
leaves of Paradise. And Adam defied his Lord, and
so went astray.
(20:117-121)

____

46 See 35:5.
47 Lit: To speak under one's breath.

Satan, by deception,[48] lured Adam and his wife beyond the safe confines of Paradise into Hell, where the tree of *zaqqum* was located. Adam and his wife could enter Hell as it was not ablaze at that time and also because Paradise and Hell are near each other. We can infer these two things because Hell will be ignited on the Day of Resurrection,[49] and because the inhabitants of Paradise and Hell will converse with each other from their respective abodes in the Hereafter.[50]

> O Children of Adam! We have sent down on you clothing to cover your bodies, and as adornment; and the clothing of godfearing – that is better; that is from the signs of God that they might reflect.
> O Children of Adam! Let not Satan tempt you as he brought your parents out from Paradise, stripping them of their clothing to show them their bodies. He sees you, he and his tribe, from where you do not see them. We made Satans as allies to those who do not believe.
>
> (7:26-27)

When their bodies were revealed to them, Adam and his wife went back to Paradise in a futile attempt to cover their nakedness, but there was no going back.

> So he directed them by deception; and when they tasted of the tree, their bodies became evident to them, so they started stitching upon themselves leaves of Paradise. And their Lord called to them, "Did I not forbid you from that tree, and say to you, 'Satan is to you a clear enemy'?"
>
> (7:22)

Adam given a second chance

God in His mercy turned to Adam and his wife in forgiveness

___

48 See 7:22.
49 See 81:12.
50 See 7:44.

and chose him.[51] Adam received words[52] from God by means of the *ruh* and was given a chance to redeem himself to, once again, be worthy of re-entering Paradise.

> Then Satan caused them to slip therefrom and brought them out of what they were in; and We said, "Get you down, some of you an enemy to some; and for you settlement and enjoyment in the land for a time."
> So Adam received words from his Lord, and He turned towards him; He is the Acceptor of repentance, the Merciful.
> We said, "Get you down from it, all together; and if guidance comes to you from Me, whoever follows My guidance, no fear shall be on them, nor will they grieve.
>
> (2:36-38)

> They said, "Our Lord, we have wronged our souls, and if You do not forgive us, and have mercy upon us, we will be of the losers."
> Said He, "Get you down, some of you an enemy to some. In the land a settlement and enjoyment for you, for a time."
> Said He, "Therein you will live, and therein you will die, and from it you will be brought out."
>
> (7:23-25)

> Then his Lord chose him, and turned to him, and guided.
> Said He, "Get you down from it, all together, some of you enemy to some; and if guidance comes to you from Me, whoever follows My guidance, he will not err, nor will he be wretched;
> And whoever turns away from My remembrance, his will be a straitened livelihood, and on the Day of

---

51 See 3:33 and 20:122.
52 Most likely a prayer for forgiveness.

Resurrection, We will gather him blind." (20:122-124)

And when We said to you, "Your Lord has encompassed[53] mankind," and We did not make the dream which we showed you and the accursed tree in the Qur'an, except as a trial for mankind. And We frighten them, but it increases them not except in great transgression.

(17:60)

In conclusion, the accursed tree *is* the tree of *zaqqum* in Hell from which Adam and his wife ate. It is a trial for mankind because those who reject its existence – by extension – reject the Hereafter. On the Day of Judgment, all of mankind will be gathered to Hell, in the midst of which grows the tree of *zaqqum*. God will deliver those upon whom He has mercy and leave the wretched to sustain themselves on the tree of *zaqqum*.

Man says, "When I am dead, am I going to be brought out alive?"
Does man not remember that We created him before, when he was nothing?
So, by your Lord, We will gather them, and the Satans, then We will present them around Hell on bent knees.
Then We will extract from every sect whichever of them was the strongest in insolence against the Almighty;
Then We will best know those deserving to burn therein.
Not one of you is there, but he will arrive at it; that is upon your Lord an inevitability decreed.
Then We shall deliver those who were godfearing; and the evildoers We shall leave there, on bent knees. (19:66-72)

---

53 To surround, grasp completely, understand fully.

3

TYRANNY 2.0

Before proceeding further, we need to clarify what the word Satan means according to the Qur'an. Satan[54] is the title of *Iblees* and means *adversary*.[55] The descendants[56] of *Iblees* are called Satans[57]. I denote those who worship Satan generically by the terms satan[58] or satans. [59]

A total war

Satan's war on man is a total war. His objective is to subjugate man in this world and lead him into Hell in the next. While some men are aware of Satan's tactics to corrupt from the inside – by whispering to man and inciting him towards evil – few are aware of his tactics to manipulate man from the outside.

Satan's strategy is based purely on deception. He deceived Adam and his wife into eating from the tree of *zaqqum* by pretending to be their sincere advisor and by playing on their fear and greed. Similarly, his tyranny deceives man by pretending to help him and by playing on his fear and greed. Satan and his tyranny have no power to benefit or harm anyone. It is all an illusion.

54 Arabic: *al-shaytan.*
55 I thank Sam Gerrans for this translated word.
56 See 7:27.
57 Arabic: *al-shayatin.*
58 Arabic: *shaytan.*
59 I give credit to Sam Gerrans for these points.

Said he, "Respite me until the day they are raised."
Said He, "You are of those that are respited."
Said he, "Because You led me astray, I shall sit in
    ambush for them on Your straight path;
Then I shall come on them from between their hands,
    and from their behind, and from their right hands
    and their left hands.[60] And You will not find most of
    them grateful."
Said He, "Go you forth from it, despised and banished.
    Whoever follows you from among them – I shall fill
    Hell with you, all together."
                    (7:14-18)

Satan is an enemy to you; so take him as an enemy.
    He only calls his party that they may be among the
    companions of the Blaze.
                    (35:6)

Let not Satan avert you; he is an open enemy to you.
                    (43:62)

Like Satan, when he said to man, "Reject"; then, when
    he rejected, he said, "I am disassociated from you. I
    fear God, the Lord of all Being."
So the outcome for both of them is that they are in the
    Fire, abiding forever therein; that is the recompense
    of the wrongdoers.
                    (59:16-17)

A match made in Hell

Since Satan's power is limited to calling man toward evil,[61]
he relies on tyrants to establish and manage his tyranny. Satan
suggests intrigue, deceit, slaughter and corruption to evil men
who lust after power and wealth. They obey his whispers,
working corruption and shedding blood. The more power they
gain, the more they increase in vileness and depravity. Satan

60 i.e. attack them on all fronts; a total war.
61 See 14:22.

29

expands his tyranny on the backs of these wretches subjugating ever greater numbers under his system. Thus, Satan and tyrants form a symbiotic relationship. This is the underlying mechanism of every tyranny.

All tyrannical empires expand until they are checked by God. Similarly, Tyranny 2.0 has reached its zenith and God's punishment is near; especially since the elites of this tyranny are now openly Satanic. They worship Satan, their god, by performing televised sacrifices – under the guise of false flag attacks[62] – and rituals – elaborate ceremonies during important events for all to see.[63]

> Said he, "My Lord, respite me until the day they are
>   raised."
> Said He, "You are of those that are respited
> Until the day of the time known."
> Said he, "Then, by Your power, I will mislead them all
>   together,
> Save Your sincere servants among them."
> Said He, "Right it is, and the Truth I say;
> I fill Hell with you, and with whoever of them follows
>   you, all together."
> (38:79-85)

Idols of Tyranny 2.0

All tyrannies comprise idols. In Tyranny 2.0, the masses worship the idols of government, medicine and religion, among others. They credit these idols for providing them with security, health, provision, help and guidance when, in truth, it is God who provides all these blessings. He alone blesses and afflicts. The Qur'an's position is clear; those who rely on idols – termed *al-taghut* – are making partners with God.

> And those who made partners say, "If God had willed,
>   we would not have worshipped; apart from Him,

62 2,977 people were sacrificed by the elites in 9/11.
63 The Super Bowl half time shows or the opening Olympic ceremonies are prime examples of these rituals.

anything, neither we nor our fathers, nor would we have forbidden, apart from Him, anything." Thus did those do from before them; so is there upon the messengers except a clear delivery?

And We had raised in every community a messenger that: "Worship God, and avoid *al-taghut*." Then among them, was he whom God guided, and among them, was he upon whom the error was justified. So journey in the land and observe how was the outcome of the deniers.

(16:35-36)

Idols lead to darkness

There is no compulsion in the faith. Righteousness has become clear from error. So whoever rejects *al-taghut* and believes in God, he has grasped the most firm handhold, unbreakable. And God is Hearing, Knowing.

God is the ally of those who believe; He brings them out from the darknesses into the light. And those who reject, their allies are *al-taghut*, they bring them out from the light into darknesses. Those are the companions of the Fire, therein abiding forever.

(2:256-257)

Right after the mention of *al-taghut,* the Qur'an relates a dispute between Prophet Abraham, a believer and an ally of God, and a king, a rejecter *and* an ally of *al-taghut.*

Have you not considered him who disputed with Abraham, about his Lord, that God had given him kingship? When Abraham said, "My Lord is He who gives life, and causes death," he said, "I give life and cause death." Abraham said, "God brings the sun from the east, so bring it from the west." Then the rejecter was confounded, and God does not guide the wrongdoing people. (2:258)

The king – an ally of the idol of power – boasted of having *illusory* power over life and death;[64] he forgot that "power belongs to God altogether".[65]

Tyranny, sorcery and idols

Tyranny, sorcery and *al-taghut* are closely related. Tyranny 2.0 uses sorcery – propaganda and illusion – to terrorize the masses keeping them in a perpetual state of awe and fear of *al-taghut* – the idols of government, religion and science – and blindly obeying its dictates.

> Have you not considered those who claim themselves
> to be pure? Nay, God purifies whom He wills, and
> they will not be wronged even a wick.
> Observe how they invent lies about God, and that is
> sufficient as a manifest sin.
> (4:49-50)

Instead of upholding the laws in the Qur'an, Muslims uphold the laws of *al-taghut*. Most of the laws in Islamic countries are derived from laws written by men.[66]

> Have you not considered those who were given a
> share of the Law, they believe in witchcraft and *al-taghut*, and say of those who rejected, "These are
> better guided than the believers as to the way"?
> Those are they whom God has cursed; and he whom
> God curses, never will you find for him a helper.
> Or have they a share in the kingdom? Then, they
> would not give mankind even a speck.
> Or are they jealous of mankind for what God has
> given them of His bounty? For We gave the house of
> Abraham the Law and wisdom, and We gave them a
> great kingdom. (4:51-54)

---

64 Illusory because no soul can die without God's permission. See 3:145.
65 2:165.
66 "Sharia." Wikipedia, Wikimedia Foundation, 23 May 2021, en.wikipedia.org/wiki/Sharia

Have you not considered those who claim that they
believe in what was sent down to you, and what was
sent down before you, desiring to go for judgment
to *al-taghut*,[67] while they have been commanded to
reject it? But Satan desires to lead them far astray.
And when it is said to them, "Come to what God
has sent down, and to the messenger," you see the
hypocrites turning away from you in aversion.
(4:60-61)

Armies fight for king and country. Tyranny 2.0 – under
the guise of defending freedom – deploys men across the
globe to spread corruption and shed blood, all for the sake of
maintaining its tyrannical system.

Those who believe fight in the way of God, and those
who reject fight in the way of *al-taghut*. So fight
against the allies of Satan; the plot of Satan is ever
weak.
(4:76)

Those who worship idols are debased

Say, "O People of the Book, do you resent us for
no other reason than that we believe in God, and
what was sent down to us, and what was sent down
before, and that most of you are rebellious?"
Say: "Shall I inform you of worse than that as
recompense with God? Whoever God has cursed
and with whom He became angry, and made of
them apes and pigs, when he worshipped *al-taghut*.
Those are worse in position and further astray from
the even way.
(5:59-60)

---

67 The current day legal system which is based on the laws of men.

God accepts repentance

And those who avoided *al-taghut*, lest they worship
them, and turn back to God, for them is good news!
So give good news to My servants
Who listen to the Word and follow the best of it.
Those are they whom God guided, and those are
men of understanding.
(39:17-18)

Tyranny 2.0 is based on fear

Once we understand that God alone has power over
everything, we break free of Tyranny 2.0's hold over us. This
mental shift allows the believers to put their trust in God alone
and resist Tyranny 2.0.

And when We said to the angels, "Submit to Adam";
so they submitted themselves, except *Iblees*. He
said, "Shall I submit myself to one You have created
from mud?"
He said, "Do You see this whom You have honored
above me? If You defer me to the Day of Resurrection,
I will master his progeny, except a few."
Said He, "Depart, for whoever of them follows
you, Hell will be your recompense – an ample
recompense.
And startle whoever you can among them with your
cry;[68] and rally against them your cavalry and your
infantry, and partner with them in their wealth and
their children, and promise them!" But Satan does
not promise them except deception.
"Over My servants you have no authority." And
sufficient is Your Lord as Trustee.
(17:61-65)

---

68 Shout, raise one's voice. Also used in 20:108, 31:19, 49:2, 49:3.

Tyranny 2.0 is global

Tyranny 2.0 is a truly global tyranny which emerged after World War II. It has many names: New Order of the Ages,[69] New World Order or One World Government. The financial engine that drives Tyranny 2.0 is usury which God has forbidden.

> Those who devour interest do not stand except like one whom Satan beats by his touch, stands. That is because they say, "Trade is like interest."[70] But God has allowed trade and forbidden interest. So whoever receives an admonition from his Lord and desists, he shall have his past gains, and his affair is with God; but whoever reverts – those are the companions of the Fire, therein abiding forever.
>
> (2:275)

By using terms such as freedom, democracy and justice, Tyranny 2.0 deceives the masses into believing that they live in a free, representative and fair society; when in reality, they live in a prison camp. This should now be obvious to any thinking men considering the usage of the term *lockdown* by the media during the scamdemic of 2020; a term which, quite recently, only meant[71] *the confining of prisoners to their cells.*[72]

Tyranny 2.0 presents a multitude of meaningless choices to the masses, all leading to the same outcome.[73] For example, every four years, it encourages the American public to perform their civic duty and vote for either a Republican or Democratic candidate to be the next President. However, the public is oblivious to the fact that both candidates are hand-picked by the same elites. It makes no difference who wins, the same agenda moves forward.

If we actually lived in a democracy, there would be a referendum on the implementation of lockdowns, mandatory

---

69 Latin: *novus ordo seclorum*; written on the U.S. dollar bill.

70 Just business.

71 Look up the term *lockdown* in any old dictionary.

72 Soanes, Catherine, and Sara Hawker. Compact Oxford English Dictionary of Current English. Oxford University Press, 2005.

73 I thank Alan Watt and Sam Gerrans for this insight.

face masks and forced injections; there was none. This fact alone should make it clear that we live in a tyranny, not a democracy. Tyrannical mandates are being forced onto the population absent any public discussion. Unfortunately, most men are oblivious to the reality of the world around them; they have "eyes with which they see not and ears with which they hear not. These are like the cattle, rather, there are further astray. These are the heedless."[74]

The tyranny of Pharaoh

The Qur'an details an ancient tyranny, the tyranny of Pharaoh, which was very similar to Tyranny 2.0 in its techniques of control. God sent prophets Moses and Aaron to Pharaoh to warn him about God's coming Judgment unless he changed course.

I shall outline, in broad strokes, their narrative as presented in the Qur'an and then proceed to highlight the similarities between the tyrannies of Pharaoh and Tyranny 2.0.

God wished to deliver the children of Israel from the tyrant Pharaoh and his council of evil men. He sent Moses and Aaron to warn him and let the children of Israel leave. Moses presented the signs of God – a staff which could turn into a snake and his right hand which shone brightly – but was rejected by Pharaoh and his council. They assumed God's signs were the same sorcery that they were using to subjugate the masses.

Pharaoh and his council devised a plan to discredit Moses and proposed a contest between him and their sorcerers. During the contest, Pharaoh's sorcerers cast their ropes and sticks bewitching the eyes of the people. Upon seeing their sorcery, Moses became fearful but God assured him and commanded him to throw his staff which "seized what they were falsifying".[75] Realizing the truth of God's signs – and Moses' mission – the sorcerers submitted to God immediately. Pharaoh was enraged and threatened them with a torturous execution, to which they replied, "To our Lord we are returning".[76]

74 7:179.
75 26:45.
76 7:125.

God afflicted Pharaoh and his people with various punishments that they might repent and change course but they persisted in their insolence and tyranny. Finally, God commanded Moses to leave the city. News of their exodus reached Pharaoh who pursued them. When his army was about to overtake Moses and his party, God intervened and commanded Moses to strike the ocean with his staff. Moses did as he was commanded and God split the ocean into two. Moses and his party crossed the ocean safely but when Pharaoh and his army tried to cross, the waves came crashing together, drowning them all. There and then, the tyranny of Pharaoh was extinguished.

I shall now highlight the similarities between Pharaoh's tyranny and Tyranny 2.0 to show you that both tyrannies comprise the same power structures and employ identical techniques to subjugate the masses. The only difference between the two is of scale and sophistication.

Rule by a Council

In Pharaoh's tyranny, power was concentrated in the hands of three men: Pharaoh, *Haman* and *Qarun*. Pharaoh was the head of a council – comprising *Haman* and *Qarun* along with other elites – which devised policies to subjugate the masses, and dealt with threats to Pharaoh's tyranny. It was the council "think-tank" that devised the strategy to hold a contest between Moses and its sorcerers in order to discredit Moses.

Similarly, power in Tyranny 2.0 is concentrated in hands of a select few, the plutocrats. They employ front men – politicians and technocrats – to impose their will on the masses. They head councils – WEF, World Bank, G20 etc. – which devise economic policies to keep the masses impoverished. They use think-tanks – Aspen Institute, RAND Corporation, CFO etc. – which brainstorm various schemes to allow the plutocrats to maintain and strengthen their grip on power.

> And We sent Moses with Our signs and a clear authority,

To Pharaoh and *Haman* and *Qarun;* they said, "A
  lying sorcerer!"
(40:23-24)

And We sent Moses with Our signs, and a clear
  authority
To Pharaoh and his Council, but they followed
  Pharaoh's command, and Pharaoh's command was
  not right-minded.
He will go before his people on the Day of
  Resurrection, and lead them into the Fire; and evil
  is the arrival arrived at.
And they are followed here by a curse, and on the
  Day of Resurrection – evil is the gift given.
(11:96-99)

A hierarchical structure

In Pharaoh's tyranny, the children of Israel occupied the
bottom rung of society. Just above them were the people of
Pharaoh, who oppressed them. The sorcerers, celebrities of
their day, occupied the middle rung. Pharaoh, *Haman* and
Qarun – the elites – occupied the highest position in the
hierarchy of Pharaoh's tyranny.

Similarly, in Tyranny 2.0, the third world populations occupy
the bottom rung of society. Just above them are the first world
populations, who oppress them. The sorcerers of our time –
actors, musicians and religious leaders – occupy the middle
rung. Billionaires, royals and politicians occupy the highest
position in the hierarchy of Tyranny 2.0.

Divide, depopulate and conquer

Pharaoh caused corruption in the land by means of a dual
strategy; he divided its people into sects – divide and conquer
– and he subjugated the children of Israel by slaughtering their
sons and raping their women – depopulation.

Similarly, Tyranny 2.0 implements the dual strategy of

divide and conquer, and depopulation on a global scale. People are being continuously divided along the lines of sex,[77] race,[78] religion[79] and ideology[80] –and, more recently, as vaxxed or unvaxxed.

Depopulation is being carried out by lowering global fertility rates – via scientific[81] and cultural[82] means – and, more recently, by mandating COVID-19 "vaccines"[83] – which cause serious side effects including infertility – for every man, woman and child on earth.

> And when Moses said to his people, "Remember God's blessing upon you when He rescued you from the family of Pharaoh, who were afflicting you with evil punishment, slaughtering your sons, and shaming[84] your women – and in that was a great test from your Lord.
>
> (14:6)

> Pharaoh exalted himself in the land and made its inhabitants into sects, weakening a party among them, slaughtering their sons, and shaming their women. He was of the corrupters.
>
> And We desired to bestow favor upon those who were weak in the land, and to make them leaders, and to make them the inheritors,
>
> And to establish them in the land, and to show Pharaoh and *Haman*, and their armies, what they were dreading through them.
>
> (28:4-6)

---

77 Feminism.
78 Racism.
79 Islam and Christianity.
80 Capitalism and Communism.
81 GMO foods and endocrine disrupters.
82 Fornication is no longer taboo, widespread use of contraception, men and women choosing to stay single.
83 Gene therapy treatments which cause infertility and deaths.
84 Usually translated as *sparing*. However, the Qur'an uses it in 2:26 and 33:53 to mean *shame* or *shy*. Historically, armies loot and rape after conquering.

A state religion

Pharaoh's tyranny had a state mandated religion. Pharaoh, being a representative of the gods in the heavens, was revered as a god on earth and worshipped by the masses.

> And he said, "I am your Lord, the exalted!"
> (79:24)

> Said he, "If you take a god other than me, I shall place you among the prisoners."
> (26:29)

Similarly, science is the mandated religion of Tyranny 2.0, and its god is the intellect. This idea might seem strange to you since you have been brought up to believe that science is the complete opposite of religion; that it is based on reason. However, science bears all the hallmarks of a religion. If it looks like a religion, swims like a religion, and quacks like a religion, then it probably *is* a religion.

- Science, like religion, has a beginning and ending mythology. It claims that the universe was created by a Big Bang and will end either in a Big Crunch or a Big Freeze.
- Science, like religion, has experts[85] who claim to understand God's laws.[86] According to their world-view, everything is based on probability and chance.
- Science, like religion, divides God's Power between its various gods. The Big Bang is the Creator. Evolution is the Fashioner. Human intellect is the Knower. All these powers are the preserve of God alone.[87]
- Science, like religion, has a code of ethics. It claims that life has no purpose. Man is free to do as he pleases.

Science claims to be agnostic when, in reality, it denies

---

85 i.e. scientists
86 Scientists are careful to use the word nature instead of God.
87 See 59:24, 6:73.

God altogether. The doctrines of this religion – atheism and materialism – are being taught to children globally[88] assimilating them into an amoralistic and atheistic world-view.

Scientists can now change the DNA of living organisms i.e. they can now change God's creation. Satan specifically stated that he would command men "so they will change the creation of God".[89]

Most of the corn, soybean and cotton grown in the U.S. is now genetically modified.[90] The development of COVID-19 "vaccines" is another insolent attempt by man to change God's creation. These gene therapies insert a synthetic mRNA code into men, women and children thereby transforming them into genetically modified organisms.[91]

> They call besides Him none but female beings; they call none but a rebellious Satan.
> God cursed him. And he said, "I will take from Your servants an ordained portion,
> And I will lead them into error, and I will arouse desires in them, and I will command them so they will cut off the cattle's ears, and I will command them so they will change the creation of God." And whoever takes Satan as an ally instead of God, he has suffered a clear loss.
> He promises them and arouses desires in them, but Satan does not promise them except deception.
>
> (4:117-120)

Haman was the religious priest in Pharaoh's tyranny.

---

88 The educational system across the world is remarkably similar in its curriculum.

89 See 4:119.

90 Center for Food Safety and Applied Nutrition. "GMO Crops, Animal Food, and Beyond." U.S. Food and Drug Administration, FDA, www.fda.gov/food/agricultural-biotechnology/gmo-crops-animal-food-and-beyond

91 I am well aware that mRNA – a subtype of RNA – is not DNA. However, the cellular machinery of the human body cannot make proteins by reading DNA directly; a fragment of it must first be decoded into mRNA, which is then used to make a protein. This gene therapy delivers synthetic mRNA to the cell thereby tricking the cellular machinery into making a custom protein. This, in effect, leads to the same outcome as the modification of the DNA of an organism.

Pharaoh ordered him to construct a tower so that he could seek the means of the heavens and discover Moses' God.[92] In Tyranny 2.0, scientists reprise the role of *Haman.*

Scientific knowledge is used to develop weapons and refine the techniques of mind control. Government organizations and elite foundations award grants to institutions such as The Chinese Academy of Sciences, Harvard University, Max Planck Society, French National Centre for Scientific Research, Stanford University and Massachusetts Institute of Technology to conduct such research.

The atomic bomb was made possible by the research of the *esteemed* professors at the University of California, Princeton University, University of Chicago and University of Virginia.   These were not naïve men; they fully understood the implications of their research. Robert Oppenheimer – considered the father of the atomic bomb – was a theoretical physicist at the University of California. He later accepted the Enrico Fermi Award presented to him by John F. Kennedy for his outstanding contribution to the building of a weapon that slaughtered thousands of Japanese men, women and children in a flash.

The elites also fund research related to psychology, pharmaceutical drugs and propaganda. Complete control over the human mind has always been the cherished goal of the elites; and they are very close to achieving it. In 1961, Aldous Huxley – the author of *Brave New World* and no stranger to the elite circles – predicted the apathetic state of today's men.

> "There will be, in the next generation or so, a pharmacological method of making people love their servitude, and producing dictatorship without tears, so to speak, producing a kind of painless concentration camp for entire societies, so that people will in fact have their liberties taken away from them, but will rather enjoy it, because they will be distracted from any desire to rebel by propaganda or brainwashing, or brainwashing

---

92 See 40:36-37.

enhanced by pharmacological methods. And this seems to be the final revolution."[93]

The elites also fund research in physics. The Large Hadron Collider, a particle accelerator built using tax payer money,[94] is used to conduct research into the building blocks of the universe. The elites want to know what makes the universe tick, so that they can control it. They seek to understand and manipulate God's created laws – while denying His existence – in order to gain complete mastery over matter.

NASA, SpaceX and the ESA have spent trillions of dollars in launching satellites and telescopes to peer into the heavens. Pharaoh wanted to peer into the heavens and ordered *Haman* to build him a tower because he wanted to discover the God of Moses.

> And Pharaoh said, "O Council, I know not for you a god other than me. Kindle for me, O *Haman*, upon the clay, and make me a tower, that I may discover[95] Moses' God; for I think he is among the liars."
> (28:38)

> And Pharaoh said, "O *Haman*, construct for me a tower, that I may seek the means, [96]
> The means of the heavens, and discover Moses' God; for I think he is a liar." And thus the evil of his work was decorated to Pharaoh, and he was diverted from the way, and Pharaoh's plot was only in ruin.
> (40:36-37)

The financial system

The elites have designed their corrupt financial system to funnel wealth upwards. Central banks, such as the Federal Reserve Board and European Central Bank, create fiat money –

---

93 Aldous Huxley, Tavistock Group, California Medical School, 1961,
94 Costing $4.75 billion, with the money coming from tax payers' pockets.
95 Look, study, inspect.
96 Means for obtaining something, reason, cause, motive.

based upon nothing – and implement economic policies causing cycles of boom and bust, siphoning the wealth generated by the masses into their coffers. The accumulation of tremendous wealth in the hands of Pharaoh and *Qarun* points to a similar system of economic exploitation in Pharaoh's tyranny.

> *Qarun* was of the people of Moses, but he oppressed them. And We had given him treasures whose keys would burden a group possessing strength. When his people said to him, "Do not exult; God does not love the exultant.
>
> But seek, through what God has given you, the abode of the Hereafter, and do not forget your portion of the world, and do good as God has done good to you. And do not seek corruption in the land; God does not love the corrupters."
>
> (28:76-77)

Use of sorcery

According to the Qur'an, sorcery means falsehood,[97] illusion[98] and witchcraft.[99] Tyranny 2.0 uses sorcery to its full effect in the form of propaganda, deception and occult symbolism via TV, film, magazines, books and the internet. Most of what the public sees has been carefully crafted to mold their perceptions.

Consider the perpetual war *of* terror which was initiated by the 9/11 false flag attack. This event – which was perpetrated by the elites – stirred the public into a frenzy of hate, anger, and vengeance. The shell shocked public actively supported the planned wars of Tyranny 2.0, which are still raging to this day.

Recently, Tyranny 2.0 has announced its plans for a Great Reset.[100] Leveraging the false narratives of climate change and a global pandemic, it is bringing in a new socio-economic

---

97 See 6:7, 10:76, 11:7, 21:3, 27:13, 28:48, 34:43, 37:15, 43:30, 46:7, 54:2, 74:24.
98 See 7:116, 20:66, 28:36, 52:15, 61:6.
99 See 2:102.
100 I refer the interested reader to a book written by Klaus Schwab, a member of the elite, titled *COVID-19: The Great Reset.*

system. The wide-scale adoption of electric cars will wean the public off of fossil fuels, lockdowns and onerous sustainable certification requirements will assure the bankruptcy of small businesses. Airports, malls and public places will require "vaccines" and "booster shots" for admission. Those who refuse to comply with the agenda will find it increasingly difficult to function in this post Great Reset society. The terrified masses will, unfortunately, go along with this seismic shift to their way of life.

Pharaoh and his council were also using sorcery to terrify the masses. When Moses brought them signs from God, they dismissed him and deceitfully cast him as an enemy to the people.

> They said, "Have you come to us to turn us away from
> that upon which we found our fathers, and that
> there be greatness in the land for you two? And we
> do not believe you.
>
> (10:78)

> They said, "These are two sorcerers desiring to drive
> you out of your land by their sorcery, and do away
> with your most exemplary way.
>
> (20:63)

Pharaoh and his council used propaganda and deception to obfuscate Moses' mission. They presented him as a terrorist who had come to drive them out from their land and destroy their fine traditions, when Moses had been clear that his only purpose was to rescue the children of Israel. Behind the scenes, they worked feverishly to come up with a plan to destroy Moses' credibility.

> Said the Council of the people of Pharaoh, "This is a
> learned sorcerer
> Who desires to drive you out from your land, so what
> do you command?"

They said, "Delay him and his brother, and send
     among the cities gatherers,
To bring you every learned sorcerer."
                    (7:109-112)

In Tyranny 2.0, actors, newscasters, religious leaders and politicians have taken up the role of the sorcerers. Using mass media, they bewitch the eyes and minds of the people confusing and terrifying them. These men and women are well versed in the craft of perception management. They keep the masses entertained, fearful and loving their servitude. Like the sorcerers of Pharaoh, they are allowed a life of luxury in return for their services.

    And the sorcerers came to Pharaoh. They said, "There
        should be a reward for us if we be the victors."
    He said, "Yes, and, you will be among the near-
        stationed."
    They said, "O Moses, either you cast, or we will be
        the casters."
    He said, "Cast," and when they cast, they bewitched
        the people's eyes, and put fear in them, and
        produced a great sorcery.
                    (7:113-116)

    And when the sorcerers came, they said to Pharaoh,
        "Is there a reward for us if we are the victors?"
    He said, "Yes, and, you will be among the near-
        stationed."
    Moses said to them, "Cast what you will cast."
    So they cast their ropes and their sticks, and said, "By
        the might of Pharaoh, we shall be the victors."
    Then Moses cast his stick, and at once it swallowed
        what they falsified;
    So the sorcerers were cast down, submitting
        themselves.
    They said, "We believe in the Lord of all Being,
    The Lord of Moses and Aaron." (26:41-48)

Thus, God eliminated the trickery of Pharaoh's sorcerers and established his signs. The sorcerers recognized the truth of God's signs as opposed to their fakery. Similarly, those who practice the art of deception in Tyranny 2.0, know that they are dealing in lies even though they have fooled the people into accepting it as the truth. Were the Qur'an presented to them in its true, original and real form,[101] they would recognize the truth in it, if God should will.

> We believe in our Lord, that He may forgive us our
> offences, and the sorcery you have forced us into.
> And God is better, and more enduring."
> (20:73)

> Said Pharaoh, "You have believed him before I gave
> you permission. He is your chief who taught you
> sorcery; so you will know. I will cut off your hands
> and feet on opposite sides, and I will impale you all
> together."
> (26:49)

> Said Pharoah, "You believed in Him before I gave you
> permission. This is a plot you plotted in the city that
> you may bring out from it its inhabitants. So you
> will know.
> I shall cut off your hands and feet on opposite sides,
> then I shall impale you all together."
> (7:123-124)

The obelisk

It should now be clear, for those who wish to see, that Tyranny 2.0 and Pharaoh's tyranny are both Satanic tyrannies; differing only in scale and sophistication. I have saved the most convincing proof for last which should remove any doubt as to the common heritage of both tyrannies.

---

101 Most translations of the Qur'an obfuscate the words of God to push the religion of Islam - the tenets of which are not found in the Qur'an.

The obelisk – a pointed, tapered structure – is found in most capital cities in the world and is regularly featured in mass media; the Washington Monument[102] being the most famous example of it.

The Washington Monument, Washington, D.C.

Image: "Washington Monument in Washington DC" by Jmarcosny, used under CC BY-SA 4.0. (https://creativecommons.org/licenses/by-sa/4.0/)

---

102 Erected in Washington, D.C.

The Arabic plural word *awtadun*, defined as *pegs, tent pins, stakes* or *poles*,[103] has a specific meaning within the Qur'an. It uses it once[104] to describe mountains, and twice[105] as something possessed by Pharaoh.

> Have We not made the earth spread out
> And the mountains, *awtadun*?
> (78:6-7)

All mountains have three characteristic features; they are fixed in the ground, are tapered and have a peak. *So al-awtadun* should also have these characteristics. The Qur'an also calls Pharaoh *the possessor of al-awtadun* in the context of imposing structures built by past tyrannies, which now lie in utter ruin.

> Have you not seen how your Lord did with *Ad*,
> And *Iram*, possessors of pillars,
> The like of which had not been created in the region?
> And with *Thamud*, who carved out the rocks in the
>   valley?
> And with Pharaoh, possessor of *al-awtadun*?
> Who transgressed in the region
> And increased therein corruption.
> So your Lord loosed upon them the whip of
>   punishment.
> (89:6-13)

We can infer from these verses that *al-awatdun* were impressive structures built by Pharaoh. There are two surviving structures from the ancient world which have captured the popular imagination, and, incidentally, share three specific features with the mountains – they are fixed in the ground, are tapered and have a peak; the pyramid and the obelisk.

---

103 Wehr, Hans, and J. Milton Cowan. A Dictionary of Modern Written Arabic (Arabic-English). Spoken Language Services, 1994.
104 As an indefinite noun (*awtadun*).
105 As a definite noun (*al-awtadun*).

Obelisk of Thutmosis I in Karnak, Egypt.

Pyramids were peppered across most of the ancient world but are not so common in the modern world.[106] In contrast, obelisks were *and* are being installed across the modern world.[107] Thus, while the pyramid and obelisk were both symbols of Satan's tyranny, the pyramid fell out of favor and the obelisk was ultimately adopted as the symbol of Tyranny 2.0.

The obelisk, defined as *a four-sided stone pillar that tapers to a point, set up as a monument or landmark,*[108] is exactly how the Qur'an uses the term *al-awtadun.*

The majority of obelisks installed all over the world were taken from Egypt; the seat of an ancient tyranny. Leaving aside the question of whether the Arabic word *firawn* – translated as Pharaoh – was the title of a ruler of an Egyptian Kingdom or a different person altogether,[109] the fact is that the Egyptian tyranny – the most ancient and well-studied tyranny of our day – took the obelisk as its symbol; the same obelisk which, in the present day, is used to mark out the domain of Tyranny 2.0.

The rules of tyrannies – past and present – imported Egyptian obelisks[110] and erected them in the capital cities of their empires. Rome, Istanbul, Paris, London and New York all have these Egyptian obelisks.

> Denied before them the people of Noah, and *Ad*, and
> Pharaoh, possessor of the obelisks.[111]
> (38:12)

---

106 The Louvre Pyramid and the Luxor Hotel are both modern representations of the pyramid.

107 "List of Obelisks." Wikipedia, Wikimedia Foundation, 17 Apr. 2021, en.wikipedia.org/wiki/List_of_obelisks.

108 Soanes, Catherine, and Sara Hawker. Compact Oxford English Dictionary of Current English. Oxford University Press, 2005.

109 I thank Sam Gerrans for this insight and refer the interested reader to his work *The Qur'an: A Complete Revelation.*

110 the earliest examples of which are found in Egypt but does not mean their design originated there; we have examples of Nubian, Assyrian and Ethiopian origin.

111 Usually translated as *pegs, stakes* or *bulwarks*. This rendering does not account for the true nature of obelisks which are set up to as monuments. See 89:10. Obelisks are now present across the land marking the dominion of Tyranny 2.0.

Every president of the United States faces this idol during his swearing in ceremony[112] proving, beyond the shadow of a doubt, the centrality of the obelisk to Tyranny 2.0.

Inaugural address of Obama from the west steps of the U.S. Capitol while facing the obelisk (visible in the horizon).

A closeup view of the obelisk during Obama's inauguration.

112 The presidential inauguration on the steps of Capitol Hill.

The erection of obelisks in all major cities today signifies that Tyranny 2.0 is now established across the entire world.

God's destruction of past tyrannies

God destroyed Pharaoh's tyranny after Moses had warned him. The same fate awaits Tyranny 2.0 once it has been warned by the believers. God's practice does not change. Until and unless the believers carry out their sacred duty of warning the leaders and followers of Tyranny 2.0, it will not be destroyed by God.[113] This idea is explored in detail in *The God Protocol*.[114]

> And We sent Moses with Our signs and a clear authority,
> To Pharaoh and *Haman* and *Qarun;* they said, "A lying sorcerer!"
> And when he brought them the truth from Us, they said, "Kill the sons of those who believe with him, and shame[115] their women." But the plot of the rejecters is only in error.
> And Pharaoh said, "Leave me to kill Moses, and let him call his Lord. I fear that he may change your faith, or that he may cause corruption to appear in the land."
>
> (40:23-26)

> And said the Council of the people of Pharaoh, "Will you leave Moses and his people to cause corruption in the land, and leave you and your gods?" Said he, "We will slaughter their sons and shame their women; and we have power over them."
>
> (7:127)

---

113 See 28:59.

114 I credit Sam Gerrans for this insight and refer the interested reader to his work *The God Protocol.*

115 Usually translated as *spare*. It also means to *embarrass* and *shame*. See 2:26, 33:53.

And Pharaoh proclaimed among his people; he said:
"O my people, do I not possess the kingdom of
Egypt, and these rivers flowing beneath me? Do you
not see?
Am I better or is this; one who is despicable and
hardly makes himself clear?
(43:51-52)

So none believed Moses, except a progeny among his
people, due to fear of Pharaoh and their Council,
that he would put them in a trial. And Pharaoh was
haughty in the land, and he was of the wanton.
(10:83)

And Moses said, "Our Lord, You have given Pharaoh
and his Council adornment and wealth in the
worldly life, our Lord, that they might lead astray
from Your way. Our Lord, obliterate their wealth,
and harden their hearts so that they will not believe,
until they see the painful punishment."
He said, "Your prayer is answered; so be upright, and
follow not the way of those who do not know."
(10:88-89)

And he was arrogant, he and his army, in the land,
against right; and they thought that they would not
be returned to Us.
So We seized him and his army, and cast them into the
sea; so observe how was the end of the wrongdoers.
And We made them leaders,[116] calling to the Fire, and
on the Day of Resurrection they will not be helped.
And We succeeded them in this world with a curse,
and on the Day of Resurrection they will be among
the vile.
(28:39-42)

116 Role models, to lead by example.

So he intended to startle them from the land, but We
drowned him and those with him, all together.
(17:103)

Tyranny 2.0 is powerless

Tyranny 2.0 – like Pharaoh's tyranny – has no power to
benefit or harm us. God *alone* has power over life and death.
No harm can come to us, unless God wills. God calls us to put
our trust in Him and gives the good news to those who follow
His guidance of victory in this life and of Paradise in the next.

Satan promises you poverty, and orders you to
indecency; but God promises you forgiveness from
Him and grace; and God is Encompassing, Knowing.
(2:268)

That is only Satan frightening his allies, so do not fear
them; but fear Me, if you are believers.
(3:175)

And when Satan decorated their works to them, and
said, "Today, no man can overcome you, for I am
a neighbor to you." But when the two hosts came
in sight of each other, he turned upon his heels,
saying, "I am disassociated[117] from you, I see what
you do not see. I fear God, and God is severe in
retribution."
(8:48)

---

117 He absolves himself of his followers.

4

THE PROMISE

The Qur'an's entire narrative is geared towards the Promised Day; a Day in which all men will be repaid in full for their works. It will be a Day of regret and sorrow for the rejecters.

> By the promised Day
> (85:2)

God makes a specific Promise in the Qur'an: that He will resurrect and recompense man for his actions on the Day. The Qur'an classifies a rejecter or a believer along the lines of acceptance or rejection of this Promise.[118] It is disbelief in the Promise of God which is at the core of why a rejecter does not fear God.

> Then how can you fear, if you rejected, a Day which
>   will make the children white-haired?
> Whereby the sky will be split, His Promise is to be
>   fulfilled.
> (73:17-18)

God's promise

Most men, on a subconscious level, are aware of the Day of Resurrection, but they put off any serious consideration of

118 Arabic: *al-waeed*

it, being distracted by the life of this world. This is a mistake. The Qur'an, repeatedly, exhorts men to take heed – to repent, reform, and work righteousness – before the arrival of the Day.

> To Him is your return, all together – God's promise,
> in truth. He originates creation, and then He repeats
> it that He may recompense those who believed and
> worked righteousness, justly. And those who reject,
> for them is a drink of boiling water and a painful
> punishment, for their rejecting.
> (10:4)

Belief or disbelief in the Day of Resurrection is the underlying reason for the opposing efforts of the believer and the rejecter. The believer's efforts are geared towards success in the Hereafter, whereas the rejecter's efforts are geared towards success in this life.

> God has promised those who believe and work
> righteousness; for them, forgiveness and a great
> reward.
> And those who rejected and denied our signs – those
> are the companions of the raging fire.
> (5:9-10)

> God has promised the hypocrite men, and the
> hypocrite women, and the rejecters, the fire of Hell,
> wherein they will abide forever. It is sufficient for
> them; and God has cursed them, and for them is a
> lasting punishment.
> (9:68)

> God has promised the believing men, and the believing
> women, gardens beneath which rivers flow, wherein
> they will abide forever, and goodly habitations in
> everlasting gardens; and good pleasure from God is
> greater; that is the great achievement.
> (9:72)

God has bought from the believers their souls and
their possessions; for that, Paradise is theirs. They
fight in the way of God; they kill, and are killed; that
is a promise binding upon Him in the Torah and the
Gospel and the Qur'an; and who fulfills his promise
better than God? So rejoice in your transaction
which you have transacted with Him. And that is
the great achievement.
(9:111)

And when Our clear signs are recited to them, you
recognize repugnance in the faces of those who
reject. They almost attack those who recite to them
Our signs. Say: "Shall I inform you of something
worse than that? The fire which God has promised
those who reject, and wretched is the place of
arrival."
(22:72)

But those who fear their Lord – for them are lofty
halls, above which are built lofty halls, underneath
which rivers flow – God's promise; God fails not
the appointment.
(39:20)

The Promise draws near

And the true Promise draws near, when the eyes of
those who rejected stare: "O woe to us! We were
heedless of this; rather, we were wrongdoers."
(21:97)

God's promise is true

Those – their shelter will be Hell, and they will find
no escape from it.
But those who believe and work righteousness – We
shall enter them into gardens beneath which rivers

flow, abiding therein forever. God's true promise;
  and who is truer in speech than God?
  (4:121-122)

Lo! God's is what is in the skies and the land. Lo! God's
  Promise is true, but most of them do not know.
He gives life and causes death, and to Him you will
  be returned.
  (10:55-56)

Those who believe and work righteousness – for
  them are gardens of Bliss
Wherein they abide forever – God's true promise;
  and He is the Exalted in Might, the Wise.
  (31:8-9)

Those are they from whom We will accept the best of
  their works, and overlook their evil deeds. Among
  the companions of Paradise – the promise of truth,
  which they were promised.
But he who says to his parents, "Fie upon you! Do
  you promise me that I shall be brought out, when
  already generations have passed away before me?"
  while they call to God for help, "Woe upon you!
  Believe; God's promise is true". But he says, "This is
  only the legends of the ancients."
Those are they upon whom the saying became Right,[119]
  among communities that have passed away before
  them, of the elites and men; they were losers.
  (46:16-18)

God's response to the rejecters

And they say, "When is this Promise, if you are
  truthful?"
Say: "I have no power to harm or benefit myself,
  except what God should will. For every community

---

119 Usually translated as *came into effect* or *binding*.

is a term; when their term comes, they cannot delay
an hour, nor can they advance."
(10:48-49)

And they say, "When is this Promise, if you are
truthful?"
If those who rejected but knew when they will be
unable to restrain the fire from their faces and from
their backs, and they will not be helped.
Rather, it will come upon them unexpectedly,
bewildering them, and they will not be able to repel
it, nor will they be respited.
(21:38-40)

And they say, "When is this Promise, if you are
truthful?"
Say: "It may be that right behind you is some of what
you are urging to hasten."
(27:71-72)

And they say, "When is this Promise, if you are
truthful?"
Say: "For you is the appointment of a Day which you
cannot delay an hour, nor can you advance."
(34:29-30)

And they say, "When is this Promise, if you are
truthful?"
They await but one blast, which will seize them while
they are arguing,
Then they will not be able to make any bequest, nor
will they return to their family.
And the Trumpet will be blown, and then from their
graves to their Lord they will come out.
They will say, "O woe to us! Who has raised us from
our sleeping place? This is what the Almighty
promised, and the envoys were truthful."

60

It is but one blast, and then they are all arraigned
  before Us.
So today no soul will be wronged in anything, and
  you will not be not recompensed except for what
  you were working.
(36:48-54)

And they say, "When is this Promise, if you are
  truthful?"
Say: "The knowledge is only with God, and I am only
  a clear warner."
So, when they see it close, the faces of those who
  rejected will be distressed, and it will be said, "This
  is what you were demanding."
(67:25-27)

Believers exhorted to be patient

So be patient; God's promise is true, and let not those
  who are uncertain incite you to treat it lightly.
(30:60)

So be patient; God's Promise is true. And ask
  forgiveness for your sin, and glorify with the praise
  of your Lord at evening and early morning.
(40:55)

So be patient; God's promise is true. And whether We
  show you some of what We promise them, or We
  cause you to die, to Us they will be returned.
(40:77)

So leave them to talk vainly and play, until they meet
  their day which they are promised.
(43:83)

God will fulfill His Promise

And the companions of Paradise will proclaim to the companions of the Fire: "We have found that which our Lord promised us true, have you found what your Lord promised you true?" They will say, "Yes." Then an announcer will announce between them: "God's curse is upon the wrongdoers
Who diverted from God's way, and sought deviation[120] therein, and were rejecters of the Hereafter."
(7:44-45)

And when it was said, "God's Promise is true; and there is no doubt of the Hour," you said, "We do not know what the Hour is; we think it is a possibility, and we are not certain."
(45:32)

And those who feared their Lord shall be driven to Paradise in groups, until, when they reach it, and its gates are opened, and its keepers will say to them, "Peace be upon you! You did well, so enter them herein abiding forever."
And they will say, "Praise be to God, who has fulfilled His Promise to us, and has bequeathed to us the land, for us to settle in Paradise wherever we will." And excellent is the reward of the workers.
(39:73-74)

God's Promise is binding upon Him

The Day when We shall roll up the sky as the rolling up of a scroll of writings. As We originated the first creation, We shall repeat it. A promise binding upon Us, We are the Doers.
(21:104)

---

120 Deviation from rectitude, insincerity

Nay, they have denied the Hour; and We have
 prepared for him who denies the Hour, a Blaze.
When it sees them from a far place, they will hear its
 raging and moaning.
And when they are cast in it, joined in a constricted
 place, there and then, they will call out for
 destruction.
"Do not call out today for one destruction, but call
 out for many destructions!"
Say: "Is that better, or the Garden of Eternity which
 is promised to the godfearing? It is for them a
 recompense and place of arrival."
They shall have whatever they will therein, abiding
 forever. A promise binding upon Him, to be
 requested.

(25:11-16)

Satan's Promise

Satan also makes a promise to his followers. But while God's
Promise is true, Satan's Promise is false. His promise to man is
the same promise that he made to Adam, that he will become
immortal and gain a dominion that does not deteriorate.[121] Of
course, Satan's promise was *and* is a deception; all souls will
taste death and everything will perish.

All that is upon the earth will perish,
But the countenance of your Lord will remain,
 Possessor of Majesty and Honor.
(55:26-27)

Adam lost all because he believed in Satan's false promise;
a stark lesson for all of us. God warned Adam not to go near
the tree of *zaqqum* by using a specific phrase, "and do not go
near."[122] This specific phrase is also used in the Qur'an to warn
us to not approach *the limits of God*,[123] beyond which lie the

121 See 7:20, 20:120.
122 See 2:35.
123 See 2:187.

sins of sexual immorality, the killing of innocent souls and the consuming of orphans' wealth.[124] Those who violate the limits of God – represented symbolically by the tree of *zaqqum* – will be the losers.[125]

Most men believe in Satan's Promise

The reason why man hoards wealth is because, on a subconscious level, he believes Satan's Promise.[126] Man steadfastly refuses to acknowledge the mounting evidence of his life's frailty – misfortune, disease and death hound him at every step. He supposes that by accumulating wealth, and by careful planning, he can escape – or, at the very least, delay – his eventual demise. Man refuses to accept the reality of his situation; that there is no escape and that God's plan is firm.[127]

> Every soul will taste death. Then to Us will you be
> returned.
>
> (29:57)

> And warn mankind of the Day when the punishment
> will come upon them, and those who did wrong
> will say, "Our Lord, respite us for a short term, we
> will answer Your call, and follow the messengers."
> "Did you not swear before, that there would be no
> decline for you?
> And you dwelt in the dwellings of those who wronged
> their souls, and it was made clear to you how We
> dealt with them, and We had presented examples
> for you."
>
> (14:44-45)

> Woe to every backbiter, slanderer,
> Who has gathered wealth and counted it
> Thinking his wealth makes him immortal. (104:1-3)

---

124 See 6:151-6:153.
125 Cf. 2:187, 2:222, 4:43, 6:151, 6:152, 17:32, 17:34.
126 That he can become immortal and gain a dominion that does not deteriorate.
127 See 68:45.

Said He, "Depart, for whoever of them follows you, Hell will be your recompense – an ample recompense.
And startle whoever you can among them with your cry;[128] and rally against them your cavalry and your infantry, and partner with them in their wealth and their children, and promise them!" But Satan does not promise them except deception.

(17:63-64)

O mankind, fear your Lord, and fear a Day when no father will avail his son, nor will a son avail his father at all. God's Promise is true, so let not the lower life deceive you, and let not the Deceiver deceive you about God.

(31:33)

O mankind, God's promise is true, so let not the worldly life deceive you and let not the Deceiver deceive you about God.

(35:5)

Satan promises you poverty, and orders you to indecency; but God promises you His forgiveness and His grace; and God is Encompassing, Knowing.

(2:268)

And they appear before God all together; and the weak say to those who were arrogant, "We were your followers, so can you avail us anything against the punishment of God?" They say, "If God had guided us, we would have guided you. It is the same for us whether we mourn, or be patient; we have no place of refuge."
And Satan says, when the matter is concluded, "God promised you a true Promise; and I promised you, but I failed you. And I had no authority over you,

---

128 Shout, raise one's voice. Also used in 20:108, 31:19, 49:2, 49:3.

65

except that I called you, and you answered me. So
do not blame me, but blame your souls; I cannot aid
you nor can you aid me. I reject your partnership
with me before. For the wrongdoers is a painful
punishment."
And those who believe, and work righteousness,
they will be admitted to gardens beneath which
rivers flow, abiding therein forever, by their Lord's
permission; their greeting therein will be: "Peace!"
(14:21-23)

On the Day of Resurrection, those who rejected will realize
that God fulfilled His promise, whereas Satan failed in his.
Their treasuries did not make them eternal sovereigns nor
prevent the decay of their dominion. On the contrary, they lost
all when they tasted death.

God's arguments for His Promise

The Qur'an presents *sound*[129] arguments to men who are
skeptical of His Promise. God created us from nothing the first
time; is our second creation more difficult than our first?

And they say, "When we are bones and crushed bits,
shall we be raised up as a new creation?"
Say: "Be you stones, or iron,
Or a creation which is harder in your estimation."[130]
Then they will say, "Who will bring us back?" Say:
"He who originated you the first time." Then they
will shake their heads at you and say, "When will it
be?" Say: "It may well be soon –
A Day He will call you, and you will respond with His
praise, and you will think you had stayed but a little."
(17:49-52)

---

129 "An argument is valid if the truth of the premises logically guarantees the
truth of the conclusion. A deductive argument is sound if and only if it is both
valid, and all of its premises are actually true. Otherwise, a deductive argument
is unsound." (Internet Encyclopedia of Philosophy, iep.utm.edu/val-snd/).
130 Lit: Or a creation of what is great in your breasts.

Do they not see that God, who created the skies and
the land, is able to create the likes of them? And He
has appointed for them a term, no doubt of it. But
the wrongdoers refuse except rejection.
(17:99)

Man says, "When I am dead, am I going to be brought
out alive?"
Does man not remember that We created him before,
when he was nothing?
(19:66-67)

Does man not see that We created him from a sperm-
drop? Then he is a clear arguer,
And he presents for Us an example and forgets his
own creation, saying, "Who will give life to bones
when they are disintegrated?"
Say: "He will give them life, who produced them the
first time, for He is Knower of all creation,"
(36:77-79)

Do they not see that God, who created the skies and
the land and did not tire by their creation, is able to
give life to the dead? Verily, He is powerful over all
things.
(46:33)

Were We worn out by the first creation? Yet, they are
in confusion over a new creation.
(50:15)

Does man think We shall not gather his bones?
Verily, We are able to fashion his fingertips.
(75:3-4)

A day of regret for the rejecters

And they have sworn by God their most strongest
oaths: God will not raise up him who dies. Rather,
it is a Promise binding upon Him, but most of
mankind know not,
That He may make clear to them that wherein they
differed, and that those who rejected may know
that they were liars.
Our word to a thing when We intend it, is only that
We say to it, "Be," and it is.
(16:38-40)

And they will be presented before your Lord in ranks.
"You have come to Us like We created you the first
time. Nay, you claimed that We did not make an
appointment for you."
(18:48)

Does he promise you that when you are dead, and are
dust and bones, that you will be brought out?
Far, Far away, is what you are promised.
It is not but our worldly life; we die and we live, and
we shall not to be raised up.
He is not but a man who has invented a lie about God,
and we will not believe him."
(23:35-38)

They said, "When we are dead, and are dust and
bones, shall we be raised up?
We have been promised this before, we and our
fathers; this is not but the legends of the ancients."
(23:82-83)

And those who reject say, "When we are dust, and
our fathers, shall we be brought out?
We have been promised this, we and our fathers
before; this is not but the legends of the ancients."

Say: "Journey in the land[131] and observe how was the
    end of the criminals."
(27:67-69)

Nay, but the Hour is their appointment, and the Hour
    is more disastrous and more bitter.
(54:46)

And the Trumpet will be blown; that is the Day of the
    threat.
(50:20)

You are only promised truthfully,
And the Faith[132] will befall.
(51:5-6)

So woe to those who reject, from their Day which
    they are promised.
(51:60)

So leave them to talk vainly and play until they meet
    their Day which they are promised,
The Day when they will come out from their graves
    quickly, as if they were hastening to an altar.
Their eyes lowered, humiliation overtaking them.
    That is the Day which they were promised.
(70:42-44)

We have warned you of a near punishment, the Day
    when a man will observe what his hands have
    forwarded, and the rejecter will say, "Oh, I wish that
    I were dust!
(78:40)

---

131 Visit your local cemetery.
132 Faith *is* recompense; men perform actions in expectation of an outcome

5

THE TRUE FAITH

The religion of Islam – not unlike other religions – claims to be divinely sanctioned. It offers *the* path to salvation claiming that unless a man converts to *Islam*,[133] he is doomed. The purveyors of Islam, however, conceal the fact that Islam is not a monolithic religion; it is divided into various hostile sects – *Sunni* and *Shia* being the dominant ones – differing markedly in their views, rites and aims. How can a divinely ordained perfect religion be fragmented into warring sects, each sect claiming to represent the true faith in the Qur'an?

The reason for this is that the true faith in the Qur'an has nothing to do with man-made sects, cults or religions, which only serve to confuse their followers about their obligations towards God. The Qur'an makes it clear that the only faith acceptable to God is man's complete surrender to Him. Subscription to a religion – Judaism, Christianity or Islam – is irrelevant.

> The faith[134] with God is surrender.[135] And those
> who were given the Law did not differ except the
> knowledge came to them, due to jealousy between

---

133 Initiation to which involves the recitation of the *shahadah* – the testification of faith; a statement not found in the Qur'an, in totem

134 Arabic: *al-din.*

135 Arabic: *al-islam*; it is an abstract noun

them. And whoever denies the signs of God, God is swift in reckoning.

So if they argue with you, say: "I have surrendered my face to God, and whoever follows me." And say to those were given the Law and the *goyim*:[136] "Have you surrendered?" And if they have surrendered, they are rightly guided; but if they turn away, then upon is only the delivery; and God is Seer of the servants.

(3:19-20)

So is it other than the faith of God they seek? And to Him has surrendered whatever is in the skies and the land, in obedience or in dislike, and to Him they will be returned.

Say: "We believe in God, and in what was sent down upon us, and what was sent down upon Abraham and Ishmael and Isaac and Jacob, and the tribes. And in what was given to Moses and Jesus, and the prophets, from their Lord; we do not differentiate between any of them, and we are in surrender to Him."

And whoever seeks a faith other than surrender,[137] it will not be accepted from him; and in the Hereafter, he will be among the losers.

(3:83-85)

Natural monotheism

Man, instinctively, knows that God alone has power. He seeks help from God when a calamity strikes. Try as tyrants might, they cannot change this instinct within man. Man is powerless and in need of God.

O mankind, it is you who are in need of God, whereas God is Self-sufficient, the Praiseworthy.

(35:15)

---

136 Those who did not inherit the Law.
137 Arabic: *al-islam*. Cf. 3:19-20

71

So set upright your face to the faith, natural
monotheism; it's[138] instinct of God, upon which
He originated mankind. There is no changing
God's creation. That is the lasting faith, but most of
mankind know not –
Turning to Him. And fear Him, and set upright the
duty, and be not of the makers of partners,
Of those who have split up their faith, and become
sects, each party rejoicing in what it has.
(30:30-32)

Prophet Abraham, a model for the believers, was an
uncompromising monotheist who turned away from all idols,
real or abstract, and worshipped God alone.

And who turns away from the religion of Abraham
except one who fools himself? And We chose him
in this world, and in the Hereafter, he will be among
the righteous.
When his Lord said to him, "Surrender," he said, "I
have surrendered to the Lord of all Being."
And Abraham bequeathed this to his sons and Jacob:
"O my sons, God has chosen for you the faith, so die
not except in surrender."
Or were you witnesses when death approached Jacob,
when he said to his sons, "What will you worship
after me?" They said, "We will worship your God
and the God of your fathers Abraham, Ishmael and
Isaac, One God; and to Him we surrender."
(2:130-133)

Say: "As for me, my Lord has guided me to a straight
path, an upright faith, the religion of Abraham,
natural monotheism; and he was not among the
makers of partners."
Say: "My duty, and my offering, and my living, and my
dying are for God, the Lord of all Being.

---

138 The soul; see: 30:28

No partner has He. And this I have been commanded,
and I am the first of those that surrender."
Say: "Shall I seek a Lord other than God when He is
Lord of all things? And each soul earns only on its
own account, and no bearer of burdens will bear
the burden of another. Then to your Lord is your
return, and He will inform you of that which you
were in difference.
(6:161-164)

And God said, "Do not take for yourselves two gods.
He is only One God; so fear only Me!"
And to Him belongs whatever is in the skies and the
land, and to Him is the lasting faith. Then will you
fear other than God?
(16:51-52)

And who is better in faith than he who surrenders his
face to God being a doer of good, and follows the
religion of Abraham, natural monotheism? And God
took Abraham for a friend.
(4:125)

Tenets of the faith

Time and again, God sent his messengers to reestablish His
covenant with the followers of His earlier revelations who
had, over time, divided themselves into sects. The messengers'
mission was to call them back to the true faith, absent any
sectarianism.

The last messenger and prophet, Muhammad, was sent
to invite the Jews and the Christians back to the true faith.
Those who heeded Muhammad's call joined a single unified
community. However, as time went on, they, again, became
divided due to mutual jealousy.[139] This is the current state of
the custodians of God's last scripture; the Qur'an.

---

139 See 3:19 and 4:88.

Those who rejected from the doctors of the law[140]
  and the makers of partners would not detach[141] until
  there came to them clear evidence.
A messenger[142] from God, reciting purified scrolls,
Therein upright Laws.
And those who were given the Law were not divided
  until after there had come to clear evidence.[143]
And they were commanded only to worship God, being
  sincere to him in the faith, natural monotheism, and
  to set upright the duty and give the purity. And that
  is the lasting faith.

(98:1-5)

The true faith has nothing to do with the complicated rules and rituals which are the bread and butter of all religions; God commands us to believe in Him and His angels, His Laws, His Messengers and the Last Day. Membership to a specific religion, cult or organization will not save us on the Day of Resurrection.

O you who believe, believe in God and His Messenger
  and the Law which He has sent down upon His
  Messenger and the Laws which He sent down
  before. And whoever disbelieves in God and His
  angels, and His Laws, and His Messengers, and the
  Last Day, has surely gone astray into far error.

(4:136)

Those who believe, and those of Jewry, and the
  Christians, and the Sabaeans – whoever believes
  in God and the Last Day and works righteousness
  – their wage is with their Lord, and no fear will be
  upon them, nor will they grieve. (2:62)

140 I thank Sam Gerrans for this translated word and refer the interested reader to his work *The Qur'an: A Complete Revelation.*

141 i.e. detach from their respective religions; Judaism and Christianity (which makes Jesus a partner with God).

142 Prophet Muhammad was sent to reestablish God's covenant with the Jews and the Christians.

143 Those who received the Law would break off into sects time after time.

If you reject, God is in no need of you, and He is not
pleased with the rejection of His servants. And if you
are grateful, He is pleased with you. And no bearer
of burdens bears the burden of another. Then to
your Lord is your return, and He will inform you
about your works. He knows what is in the breasts.
(39:7)

6

MAKING PARTNERS WITH GOD

God does not forgive the making of partners with Him. Considering the gravity of this sin, we must be clear on what making a partner – or partners –means in the theology of the Qur'an.

> God does not forgive the making of a partner with Him, but He forgives other than that for whom He wills. And whoever makes a partner with God, he has gone astray into far error.
>
> (4:116)

> They have rejected who say, "God is the Messiah, son of Mary." While the Messiah said, "O Children of Israel, worship God, my Lord and your Lord. Whoever makes a partner with God, God has forbidden the Paradise for him, and his shelter is the Fire; and the wrongdoers will have no helpers."
> They have rejected who say, "God is the third of three." There is no god but One God. And if they do not desist from what they say, there will touch those who have rejected among them a painful punishment.
>
> (5:72-73)

Is He who creates like one who does not create? Will
   you not consider?

(16:17)

Say: "Who is Lord of the skies and the land?" Say:
   "It is God." Say: "Have you taken other than Him
   allies who possess for themselves neither benefit
   nor harm?" Say: "Are the blind and the seeing
   equal? Or, are the darknesses and the light equal?
   Or, do they make for God partners, who create like
   His creation, so that both creations look similar to
   them?" Say: "God is the Creator of everything, and
   He is the One, the Omnipotent."

(13:16)

It will be proclaimed to those who rejected, "God's
   abhorrence of you is greater than your abhorrence
   of yourselves, when you were called to faith, but
   you rejected."
They will say, "Our Lord, twice have You caused us
   to die, and twice have You given us life; now we
   confess our sins. Is there any way out?"[144]
That is because, when God was called to alone, you
   rejected; but if partners were made with Him, then
   you believed. So the Judgment belongs to God, the
   Exalted, the Great.

(40:10-12)

According to Muslims' understanding, making a partner – or
partners – with God means to associate a deity – or deities –
with Him. The Qur'an confirms this to be the case, however,
when we carefully study the usage of *making partners with
God* in the Qur'an, we realize that, on a deeper level, this term
is closely tied to the dual concepts of *power* and *trust.*

Every man whether he is an atheist, Muslim, Christian
or Hindu places his trust in something.[145] Those who make
partners with God place their trust in their partners. They

144 Lit: So is there to get out any way?
145 I thank Sam Gerrans for this insight.

77

believe that their partners have the power to benefit or harm them, and trust them to come to their aid in a crisis. A believer, on the other hand, believes that only God has the power to benefit or harm him and, unlike the makers of partners, places his trust solely in God. Armed with this insight, we can see why most men are makers of partners with God, though they claim otherwise.

> And most of them do not believe in God except while
>   making partners.
>
> (12:106)

> There is no compulsion in the faith. Righteousness
>   has become clear from error. So whoever rejects *al-*
>   *taghut* and believes in God, he has grasped the most
>   firm handhold, unbreakable. And God is Hearing,
>   Knowing.
>
> (2:256)

> Say: "Journey in the land and observe how was the
>   outcome of those that were before; most of them
>   were makers of partners."
> So set upright your face to the lasting faith before
>   there comes from God a day of which there is no
>   repelling. On that day, they will be divided.
> (30:42-43)

Usually, when men encounter a crisis they call to God for help. However, once it passes, they usually attribute their success to their "smarts", Luck,[146] or other men.

> And when they board the ships, they call to God,
>   being sincere to Him in the faith. But when He has
>   delivered them to the land, then they make partners,
> To reject what we gave them and to enjoy themselves;[147]
>   but they will come to know. (29:65-66)

---

146 Lady Luck. The roman goddess of fortune; Fortuna.

147 After a perceived danger has passed, they carry on transgressing God's commands. See 10:23.

It is He who created you from one soul, and created
from it its pair that he might rest in her. Then, when
he covers her, she carries a light burden – passing
by with it. Then, when she grows heavy, they call to
God, their Lord, "If You should give us one sound,
we will be of the grateful."
But when He gives them one sound, they make
for Him partners in what He has given them; but
exalted is God above what they make partners.
Do they make partners that which does not create
anything and are themselves created,[148]
And are neither able to help them, nor help
themselves?

(7:189-192)

And when hardship touches mankind, they call to
their Lord, turning to Him. Then when He lets them
taste mercy from Him, then a faction of them makes
partners with their Lord,
To reject what We have given them. So enjoy
yourselves, you will come to know.

(30:33-34)

The Qur'an gives us specific characteristics of those who
make partners with God; for it is not what a man claims, but his
actions, that define him.

Separating from the true faith

As we discussed earlier, the true faith – surrender to God –
is an altogether different concept from the polluted, corrupted
and compromised man-made religions masquerading as
guidance from God. In reality, religions are setup by evil men
to serve their interests. The followers of a religion are directed
into performing useless rituals, and to follow the dictates of
priests, rabbis and *imams* – most of whom are corrupt, greedy[149]

148 This is not a grammatical error; the Qur'an is covering both positions: making
a partner with God, and making partners with God.
149 See 9:34.

79

or serve the interests of the elites. Throughout history, tyrants have used religions to control the masses by encouraging passivity and groupthink, and discouraging independent action and personal responsibility. In contrast, the true faith frees a believer from the oppression of religions and encourages him to take action against the oppressors of mankind. It bestows inalienable rights upon a man from God Himself.

> Those who divided their faith and became sects, you
> are not of them in anything. Their affair is only unto
> God, then He will inform them about what they
> were doing.
> Whoever comes with good deed will have ten the like
> of it; and he who comes with evil deed will not be
> recompensed except the like thereof; and they will
> not be wronged.
> (6:159-160)

> The companions of the Fire will call to the companions
> of Paradise: "Pour upon us some water, or some of
> what God has provided you!" They will say: "God
> has forbidden them to the rejecters
> Who took their faith as a distraction and a game, and
> whom the lower life deceived." So today, we forget
> them as they forgot the meeting of this Day of theirs,
> and their striving against Our signs.
> (7:50-51)

At the time of Prophet Muhammad, both Jews and Christians claimed to be following Prophet Abraham – their common patriarch. This is also the claim of the religion of Islam today. The Qur'an points out that Abraham was neither a Jew nor a Christian – and by extension, nor was he a *Muslim*; he simply surrendered to God.

> And they say, "Be Jews or Christians and you will be
> guided." Say: "Nay, the religion of Abraham, natural

monotheism, and he was not of the makers of
partners."
Say: "We believe in God, and in what was sent down
to us and what was sent down upon Abraham and
Ishmael and Isaac and Jacob, and the tribes. And in
what was given to Moses and Jesus, and what was
given to the prophets, from their Lord; we do not
differentiate between any of them, and we are in
surrender to Him."
So if they believe similar to what you believe in, then
they are guided; but if they turn away, then they are
clearly in schism; and God will be sufficient for you
against them; and He is Hearing, the Knowing.
(2:135-137)

The claim of the Jews, Christians – and Muslims – that a
man is only guided if he follows their religion is refuted by
the Qur'an. The fact of the matter is that Jews, Christians and
Muslims have all separated from the true faith, "each party
with what is with them, rejoicing".[150] Those who break off from
the true faith and setup their own religions, sects or creeds
are those who make partners with God; they have chosen to
follow the guidance of their ancestors, leaders or their own
vain desires in preference to God's guidance.

And when it is said to them, "Follow what God has
sent down," they say, "Rather, we shall follow that
upon which we found our forefathers." What?
Even though Satan was calling them to the blazing
punishment?
(31:21)

He has ordained for you of faith what He enjoined
upon Noah, and that We have inspired to you, and
what We enjoined upon Abraham, Moses and Jesus
that you set upright the faith and be not divided
therein. Difficult for the makers of partners is what

---

150 30:32

you call them towards. God chooses for Himself
whoever He wills, and guides to Himself whoever
turns.

And they did not split until after knowledge had come
to them, out of mutual jealousy. And had it not been
for a preceding Word from your Lord until a stated
term, it would have been decided between them.
And those who inherited the Book after them, they
are uncertain of it, in doubt.

(42:13-14)

Religionists do not follow Prophet Abraham

The Jews, Christians and Muslims all claim to follow the
religion of Abraham i.e. each of them claims that Prophet
Abraham was familiar with the implementation details of his
respective religion.

Say: "O doctors of the law![151] Come to an equal word
between us and you, that we worship none but God,
and that we do not partner anything with Him, and
that some of us do not take some as Lords other
than God." But if they turn away, say: "Bear witness
that we are in surrender."

O doctors of the law! Why do you argue about
Abraham, when the Torah and the Gospel were not
sent down until after him? Do you not reason?

You are the ones who argue about what you know,
but why do you argue about what you do not know?
And God knows, and you know not.

Abraham was neither a Jew nor a Christian, but he
was a natural monotheist, in surrender; and he was
not of the makers of partners.

The people closest to Abraham are those who
followed him, and this Prophet, and those who
believe; And God is the Ally of the believers.

(3:64-68)

---

151 I credit Sam Gerrans for this translated phrase.

However, the verses above are arguing the opposite of the religionists' claim. At the time of Abraham, the Torah and Gospel – and obviously, the Qur'an – had not been revealed, so how could he be aware of the implementation details of any of these religions? Even if we ignore the fact that the major doctrinal pillars[152] of these religions are derived from sources[153] other than their respective Scriptures, how could Abraham – who had not studied any of these Scriptures – implement the commandments and rituals unique to each religion?

But Abraham did surrender to the Lord of all Being. Thus anyone who wishes to follow Abraham – who is a role-model in the Qur'an – need only to surrender to God; conversion to any specific religion is not required. This is the meaning of the word *muslim*, one who surrenders to God.

> When his Lord said to him, "Surrender," he said, "I
> have surrendered to the Lord of all Being."
> (2:131)

God's argument given to Abraham

> And when Abraham said to his father *Azar*, "Do you
> take idols for gods? I see you, and your people, in
> clear error."
> And thus did We show Abraham the kingdom of the
> skies and the land, that he might be of those having
> certainty:
> When the night covered him, he saw a planet.[154] He
> said, "This is my Lord." But when it set, he said, "I
> love not the setters."
> And when he saw the moon rising, he said, "This is
> my Lord." But when it set, he said, "Unless my Lord
> guides me, I shall be of the erring people."

---

152 The five pillars in the case of Islam.
153 The *hadith* literature and *Sunnah*, in the case of Islam.
154 Probably Venus since it shines the brightest right after dusk; usually translated as star.

And when he saw the sun rising, he said, "This is my
  Lord; this is greater!" But when it set, he said, "O
  my people, I am free from what you make partners.
I have turned my face to Him who split the skies and
  the land, natural monotheism; and I am not of the
  makers of partners."
And his people argued with him. He said, "Do you
  argue with me about God when He has guided me?
  And I do not fear what you make partners with
  Him, save that my Lord should will anything. My
  Lord embraces all things in knowledge; will you not
  reflect?
And how should I fear what you have made partners
  when you do not fear having made partners with
  God that for which He has not sent down upon you
  any authority? So which of the two factions has
  more right to security, if you should know?
Those who believe, and do not mix their belief with
  wrongdoing – theirs is security; and they are guided.
And that is our Our argument, which We gave to
  Abraham against his people. We raise up in degrees
  whom We will. Your Lord is Wise, Knowing.
                    (6:74-83)

Abraham's argument to his people – which was given to
him by God – was that he had no reason to fear their claimed
partners of God because those who invented this lie did not
fear the wrath of God, the Almighty. Hence, we come to the
core characteristic of the *makers of partners*, instead of fearing
God, they fear others besides Him.

Cast a look around you, can you sincerely state that most of
those who claim to believe in God are not *makers of partners*?
Do they fear God alone? Most men – whether they call
themselves Jews, Christians or Muslims – live their lives in fear
of other more powerful men. They acquiesce to the wrongful
orders of authority figures fearing the loss of livelihood, wealth
and respect. They live in terror of Tyranny 2.0.

Wealth and children

It is natural for man to seek wealth and children as they are natural sources of enjoyment and content. "Wealth and sons are the decoration of the lower life."[155] However, God exhorts us to beware of them, as they are a trail. We must trust and rely solely upon God.

Satan partners with man through his wealth and children giving him the false hope that they can help and protect him. The truth is that only God is our Ally and Protector.

> All that is upon the earth will perish,
> But the countenance of your Lord will remain, Possessor of Majesty and Honor.
> (55:26-27)

> And when We said to the angels, "Submit to Adam"; so they submitted themselves, except *Iblees*. He said, "Shall I submit myself to one You have created from mud?"
> He said, "Do You see this whom You have honored above me? If You defer me to the Day of Resurrection, I will master his progeny, except a few."
> Said He, "Depart, for whoever of them follows you, Hell will be your recompense – an ample recompense.
> And startle whoever you can among them with your cry;[156] and rally against them your cavalry and your infantry, and partner with them in their wealth and their children, and promise them!" But Satan does not promise them except deception.
> "Over My servants you have no authority." And sufficient is Your Lord as Trustee.
> (17:61-65)

---

155 18:46.

156 Shout, raise one's voice. Also used in 20:108, 31:19, 49:2, 49:3.

The man with the two gardens

And present to them an example: two men. We made for one of them two gardens of grapevines, and surrounded them with palm trees, and made between them a sown field;

Each of the two gardens brought forth its produce and did not fail in anything; And We caused a river to gush forth therein.

And he who had fruit said to his companion, when he was conversing with him, "I am more than you in wealth, and greater in group."

And he entered his garden, when he was wronging his soul. He said, "I do not think that this will ever perish

And I do not think the Hour will occur; and if I am returned to my Lord, I will find better than this in exchange."

His companion said to him, when he was conversing with him, "Do you reject Him who created you from dust, then from a sperm drop, then fashioned you a man?

But as for me, He is God, my Lord, and I do not partner with my Lord anyone.

And why, when you entered your garden, did you not say, "Whatever God wills, there is no strength except iñ God"? If you see me inferior to you in wealth and children,

Then it may be that my Lord will give me better than your garden, and will send upon it a reckoning from the sky, so that it becomes a slippery plateau,

Or its water runs off underground, so you are unable to seek it."

And his fruits were encompassed, gand he began wringing his hands over what he spent on it, while it was collapsed upon its trellises, and he was saying, "Oh, would that I had not partnered with my Lord anyone!"

But there was no group to help him, other than God,
and he could not help himself.
There and then, protection belongs only to God, the
True. He is best in reward and best in outcome.
(18:32-44)

The man with the two gardens never claimed that God had
a partner nor did he call to anyone besides God. Yet, in his
anguish he cries out, "O, would that I had not partnered with
my Lord anyone!" He did, however, boast about his wealth
and numbers thinking they would not perish. He trusted in the
resources granted to him by God and received a humiliating
schooling in the end.

If a man believes that his wealth and children can protect
or help him, then he is making them a partner with God.
Protection belongs to God alone and only He is to be relied
upon. "But there was no group to help him, other than God, and
he could not help himself."

Trusting might

Throughout history, tyrants have always relied upon military
might as the ultimate safeguard. Similarly, the elites of Tyranny
2.0 count on their air, land and naval forces to defend them
against any eventuality. They forget that nothing can defend
against God's might.

Have they not journeyed in the land and observed
how the outcome of those before them was? They
were more populous than them and greater in
strength and in imprint on the land; yet what they
acquired[157] did not benefit them.
And when their messengers came to them with clear
signs, they exulted in what knowledge they had, but
they were surrounded by what they were ridiculing.

---

157 Has a connotation of knowledge which is alluded to in the next verse.

Then, when they saw Our might, they said, "We
   believe in God alone, and we reject what we were
   making partners with Him."
But their belief did not benefit them when they
   saw Our might – the tradition of God which has
   preceded for His servants – there and then, the
   rejecters lost.

(40:82-85)

Trusting men

The media constantly brainwashes the public into believing
that powerful and wealthy men are working tirelessly to save
mankind from the next great calamity.[158] Nothing could be
further from the truth. These exploiters are not laboring to help
mankind, but to enslave it. It is no secret that these tycoons
have accumulated their wealth on the backs of millions of
impoverished workers. These "philanthropists" use deceptive
charities, foundations and public-private partnerships to
implement long terms agendas which destabilize societies,
destroy sovereign nations and kill independent businesses.
Their end goal is to control all the resources on the planet.

And the Day when We shall gather them all together,
   then We shall say to those who made partners:
   "Where are your partners whom you were claiming?
Then, their only trial will be that they will say, "By
   God, our Lord, we were never makers of partners."
Observe how they lie against their souls, and what
   they were inventing has led them into error.[159]

(6:22-24)

On the Day of Judgment, the defense of the makers of
partners would be that they were not *makers of partners* i.e.
they were deceived themselves! But, the truth of the matter is
that they *were* makers of partners[160] because they believed that

158 Climate change, overpopulation and pandemics.
159 See 3:24, 6:138, 7:53, 11:21, 16:87, 28:75, 46:28.
160 See 12:106

88

others besides God could help them.

> And the Day when He will call to them, and say,
> "Where are My partners whom you were claiming?"
> Those upon whom the Word will be justified will
> say, "Our Lord, these whom we led astray, we led
> them astray even as we ourselves were astray. We
> clear ourselves to You; it was not us that they were
> worshipping."
> And it will be said, "Call to your partners!" So they
> will call to them, but they will not respond to them,
> and they will see the punishment, had they but been
> guided.
>
> (28:62-64)

Those who make partners with God attribute intercession, the power to intervene on their behalf on Judgment Day, to men. Christians claim that Jesus Christ will intercede on their behalf while Muslims claim the same for Muhammad. The Qur'an informs us what Jesus and Muhammad will say on the Day of Judgment.

> And when God will say, "O Jesus, son of Mary, did
> you say to men, 'Take me and my mother as gods
> besides God'?" He will say, "Glory be to You! It was
> not for me to say to which I had no right. If I had
> said it, You would have known it. You know what is
> in my soul, and I do not know what is in Your soul.
> You are the knower of the unseen.
> I only said to them what You commanded me:
> 'Worship God, my Lord and your Lord.' And I was
> a witness over them as long as I was with them;
> but when You took me, You were the Watcher over
> them; You are Witness over all things.
> If You punish them, they are Your servants, and if
> You forgive them, You are the Exalted in Might, the
> Wise."
>
> (5:116-118)

And the messenger will say, "O my Lord, my people
took this Qur'an as absurd."[161]
(25:30)

None has the power to intercede before God without His
permission.[162]

"And you have come to Us alone, as We created you
the first time, and you have abandoned what We
conferred upon you behind your backs. And We
do not see with you your intercessors, those you
claimed were partners with you. There is a severance
between you, and what you were claiming has led
you into error."
(6:94)

Men worship power. Tyranny 2.0, ultimately, derives its
illusory[163] power from its display of force. The masses fear and
obey the wielders of these instruments of warfare. But, the
truth is "that power is to God altogether and that God is strong
in punishment."[164] He, alone, is to be feared and obeyed.

And startle whoever you can among them with your
cry;[165] and rally against them your cavalry and your
infantry, and partner with them in their wealth and
their children, and promise them!" But Satan does
not promise them except deception.
(17:64)

And among mankind is one who sets up rivals to
God;[166] they loving them like the love for God, but
those who believe are stronger in love for God.

---

161 The primary idea is that they treated it as an archaic book, not relevant to
their day and age.
162 See 2:255.
163 Men think it to be powerful, but those with knowledge know that power
belongs to God alone.
164 2:165.
165 Shout, raise one's voice. Also used in 20:108, 31:19, 49:2, 49:3.
166 Lit: who takes rivals other than God.

If only the wrongdoers could see, when they will
see the punishment, that power belongs to God
altogether, and that God is strong in punishment.

When He will separate the followed from the
followers, and they will see the punishment, and
the relations between them will be cut off,[167]

And those who followed will say, "If only we had
another turn, we would separate from them as they
have separated from us!" Thus God will show them
their works to them as regrets, and they will not
come out from the Fire.

(2:165-167)

Trusting Satan

And they will appear before God all together; and the
weak will say to those who were arrogant, "We were
your followers, so can you avail us anything against
the punishment of God?" They will say, "If God had
guided us, we would have guided you. It is the same
for us whether we mourn, or be patient; we have no
place of refuge."

And Satan will say, when the matter is concluded,
"God promised you a true Promise; and I promised
you, but I failed you. And I had no authority over
you, except that I called you, and you answered
me. So do not blame me, but blame your souls; I
cannot aid you nor can you aid me. I reject your
partnership with me before. For the wrongdoers is
a painful punishment."

(14:21-22)

On the Day of Judgment, Satan will respond to his followers,
"I cannot aid you nor can you aid me. I reject your partnership
with me before." The followers of Satan, those who serve
Tyranny 2.0, were not only relying on Satan to come to their
aid but that they were also expected to come to his aid. It was

---

167 Lit: severed between them are the causes.

a relationship of reciprocity. This is precisely the relationship
a tyranny has with its subjects. Thus, those who rely and trust
Tyranny 2.0, other men, their riches or anything else besides
God are in *partnership with Satan.*

> So when you recite the Qur'an, seek refuge in God
> from the outcast Satan;
> He has no authority over those who believe and trust
> in their Lord;
> His authority is only over those who entrust him[168]
> and those who partner with him.
>
> (16:98-100)

Glorifying prophets

The religions of Judaism, Christianity and Islam all glorify
their respective prophets over others. The Qur'an is clear, all
prophets and messengers were the servants of God, and the
believers are not to differentiate between any of them.[169] Only
God has the right to be glorified and He alone has the power to
cause benefit or harm.[170]

> Say: "Have you seen that which you call to other than
> God? Show me what they have created of the land;
> or have they a partnership in the skies? Bring me a
> book before this, or a remnant of knowledge, if you
> are truthful."
> And who is further in error than he who calls to
> other than God, one who responds not to him until
> the Day of Resurrection, and are heedless of their
> calling,
> And when mankind is gathered, will be hostile to
> them, and will reject their worship.
>
> (46:4-6)

---

168 With their affairs.
169 See 3:84.
170 See 21:26, 5:116.

And they worship other than God what neither harms
them nor benefits them, and they say, "These are
our intercessors with God." Say: "Will you inform
God of what He does not know in the skies or in
the land?' Glory be to Him, and Exalted is He above
what they make partners.

(10:18)

And the Day We will gather them all together, then
will We say to those who made partners: "In your
places, you and your partners." Then We will
separate them, and their partners will say, "You
were not worshipping us,
And God is sufficient as a witness between us and you
that we were heedless of your worship."

(10:28-29)

Say: "Is there of your partners one who originates
creation, then repeats it?" Say: "God originates
creation, then repeats it; so how deluded are you?"
Say: "Is there of your partners one who guides to the
truth?" Say: "God guides to the truth; so is He who
guides to the truth more worthy to be followed, or
he who guides not unless he be guided? What then
is the matter with you, how do you judge?"

(10:34-35)

Dividing the Qur'an

Muslims divide the Qur'an into two parts, one revealed in
Mecca, and the other revealed in Medina. They assign foreign
definitions – via the *hadith* literature – to Qur'anic terms in
order to justify their invented rituals and create a foundation
for their religion.[171] By these means, the Muslims divide the
Qur'an, a monolithic and integrated Scripture, into disjointed
and unrelated bits which they then claim can only be understood
by means of the *hadith* literature.

---

171 I thank Sam Gerrans for these insights.

And say: "I am a clear warner."
As We have sent down upon the dividers.
Those who have made the Qur'an into portions,
Now, by your Lord, We shall question them all
together
About what they were doing.
So declare what you are commanded and turn away
from the makers of partners.
We are sufficient for you against the mockers,
Those who make with God another god.[172] But they
are going to know.

(15:89-96)

They inhabit God's temples

It is not for the makers of partners to inhabit God's
temples, bearing witness against themselves of
their rejection. Those, their works are futile, and
they will remain in the Fire forever.
Only he inhabits God's temples who believes in God
and the Last Day, and sets upright the duty, and
gives the purity, and fears not save God; and it may
be that those are among the guided.

(9:17-18)

Making religious leaders as partners with God

Religious leaders deceive their followers by commanding
them to perform invented rituals and obey man-made rules,
when, in fact, most of these injunctions are not present in
their divinely revealed Scriptures. All religious leaders – be
they popes, priests, rabbis, *imams* or *muftis* – have two things
in common, they claim to guide men and they claim to have
legislative authority.[173] However, the Qur'an categorically

---

172 They have taken their vain desires as a god. See 45:23.
173 In Islamic tradition, a *mufti* is a legal expert empowered to give rulings on
religious matters. While he claims to derive rulings from the Qur'an, most of
these rulings are, instead, derived from the *hadith* literature; in effect supplanting
God's Laws with man's laws.

denies both of these privileges to them; only God guides to the right path and only God gives rulings.[174]

We see a parallel between the offerings made by *the makers of partners* in the Qur'an and the grain offering in the religion of Judaism: "An offering of fine flour or unleavened baked goods, mixed with oil. A handful of the offering was burned (with incense) in the altar fire. The rest went to the priests."[175] The implication being that the priests were *in effect* being made partners with God.

> And they make for God a portion of what He multiplied of tilth and cattle, saying: "This is for God", according to their claim, "and this is for our partners." But, what is for their partners does not reach God and what is for God reaches to their partners. Evil is what they judge.
>
> (6:136)

The priests of the Aztec religion made fair the killing of their children to many of the *makers of partners*. Child sacrifice was common in Pre-Columbian cultures[176] with religious leaders presiding over this abominable ritual.

> And thus their partners make fair the killing of their children to many of the makers of partners, and confuse their faith for them. And had God willed, they would not have done so; so leave them and that which they invent.
>
> (6:137)

By obeying the dictates of religious leaders in lieu of the dictates of God, men have taken these priests, rabbis or imams as partners besides God.

---

174 I thank Brother Gerrans for this point. See 4:176, 5:48, 12:40, 24:1.

175 "Sacrifice in Ancient Israel by William K. Gilders." Sacrifice in Ancient Israel, www.bibleodyssey.org/en/passages/related-articles/sacrifice-in-ancient-israel.

176 "Human Sacrifice in Pre-Columbian Cultures." Wikipedia, Wikimedia Foundation, 8 Feb. 2021, en.wikipedia.org/wiki/Human_sacrifice_in_pre-Columbian_cultures

The truth of the matter is that most religious leaders misguide the masses. An *imam* diverts his followers from the Qur'an when he insists that the *hadith* literature be used to explain, add or abrogate the Qur'an; a Scripture which, itself, claims to be an explanation.[177] He leads his followers astray when he allows or forbids other than what God has allowed or forbidden.

> Fight those who do not believe in God and the Last Day and do not forbid what God and His messenger have forbidden and do not yield to the true faith from those who were given the Law until they give tribute[178] and are humiliated.
>
> And the Jews say, "Ezra is the Son of God"; and the Christians say, "The Messiah is the Son of God." That is the utterance of their mouths, they imitate the saying of those who rejected before. God curses them; how deluded are they?
>
> They have taken their rabbis and their priests as lords other than God, and the Messiah, son of Mary. And they were not commanded except to worship One God; there is no god but Him. Exalted is He above what they make partners
>
> Desiring to extinguish God's light with their mouths; but God refuses but to perfect His light, though the rejecters dislike it.
>
> It is He who sent His messenger with the guidance and the true faith to manifest it over every faith, though the makers of partners dislike it.
>
> O you who believe, many of the rabbis and religious scholars devour the wealth of mankind in vanity and divert from the way of God. And those who hoard gold and silver, and spend it not in the way of God – give them good news of a painful punishment,
>
> The day when it will be heated in the fire of Hell, and their foreheads and their sides and their backs will

---

177 See 12:111, 17:12.
178 Lit: repayment from their hands

be branded with it: "This is what you hoarded for yourselves, so taste what you were hoarding."
(9:29-35)

Or have they partners, who ordain for them of the faith that which God has not given permission for? And were it not for the Decree of Judgment, it would have been decided between them. For the wrongdoers is a painful punishment.
(42:21)

And who is more unjust than he who forges a lie about God, when he is being called to surrender?[179] And God does not guide the wrongdoing people.
They desire to extinguish God's light with their mouths; but God will perfect His light, though the rejecters dislike it.
It is He who sent His messenger with the guidance and the true faith to manifest it over every faith, though the makers of partners dislike it.
(61:7-9)

It is He who sent His messenger with the guidance and the true faith to manifest it over every faith; and God is sufficient as a Witness.
(48:28)

Some of the Jews take words out of context[180] and say: "We have heard and we disobey" and "Hear other than what is heard" and "Heed us," complicating[181] with their tongues and defaming the faith.[182] And had they said, "We heard and we obey" and "Hear and respite us,"[183] it would have been better for

---

179 Arabic: *al-islam.* Cf. 3:19-20.
180 Lit: they distort words from their places.
181 Lit: twisting with their tongues; making simple things complicated.
182 They make mockery of God's faith which is reasonable and simple to implement.
183 Give us time to understand and implement.

them, and more upright; but God has cursed them
for their rejection, so they believe not except a few.
(4:46)

7

WORSHIP OF GOD

Every religion worships its deity differently. A Hindu worships *Hanuman* by chanting the *Hanuman Chalisa,* a Christian worships his Trinitarian god by singing hymns, and a Muslim worships *Allah* by performing a ritualistic prayer which he conflates with the *al-salaat* in the Qur'an. But how does God want us to worship Him? Muslims usually cite the following verse in defense of their worship of *Allah*:

> And they were not commanded except to implore
> God, being sincere to him in the Faith,[184] natural
> monotheism, and to set upright *al-salaat* and to
> give the purity. And that is the lasting Faith.
> (98:5)

However, the Qur'an's usage of the term *al-salaat* is completely at odds with Muslims' understanding of *al-salaat* as a ritualistic prayer.

Al-salaat means duty

Muslims claim that *al-salaat* is a ritual – comprising a set

---

184 The phrase: being sincere to Him in the Faith is attached in this only one instance with worshipping God, the rest of the time it is attached to calling God. See 7:29,10:22,29:65,31:32,40:14,40:65. The implication is that they are closely related.

order of specific movements – which is performed in the direction of the *Kaaba* at specific times throughout the day (and night). Such a rigid definition of *al-salaat* is impossible to reconcile with its usage in the Qur'an.

Firstly, the Qur'an does not give us the specifics of this ritual; which it must, if it is true to its claim of being clear, complete and detailed.[185]

Secondly, even if we accept the Muslims' standard response that the Qur'an mentions *sujud* and *rukuh* – which they claim to mean the actions of prostration and bowing in their ritual prayer – we are still unable to reconstruct their complete ritual prayer using the Qur'an exclusively.

Finally, by insisting that *al-salaat* means a ritual prayer, Muslims are inadvertently claiming that God and His angels perform a ritual prayer! Of course, such a thing is impossible, but that is the inescapable conclusion if we consider an atypical traditional translation.

> While he was standing in *prayer (yusalli)*[186] in the chamber, the angels called unto him: "Allah doth give thee glad tidings of Yahya, witnessing the truth of a Word from Allah, and (be besides) noble, chaste, and a prophet,– of the (goodly) company of the righteous."
>
> (3:39)

In the above verse, Abdullah Yusuf Ali renders the Arabic word *yusalli* – which is derived from the same root as *al-salaat, s-l-w* – as *prayer*. However, in the verse below where the context is of God and the angels,[187] he translates *yusalluna* – a plural of *yusalli* – as *send blessings.* If he was consistent in his translation, he would translate *yusalluna* as *they do prayer*, but that would be highly inappropriate considering that the subject is God and His angels.

---

185 See 14:52, 6:115, 17:12.
186 Lit: he does *al-salaat.*
187 See 33:56.

Allah and His angels *send blessings (yu-salluna)* [188] on
the Prophet: O ye that believe! *Send ye blessings
(sallu)* [189] on him, and salute him with all respect.
(33:56)

Unfortunately, all translators – with the exception of Sam
Gerrans – employ such sleighs of hand when translating key
terms in the Qur'an.

The facts are that *al-salaat* is a general term which simply
means *duty*[190] and the specifics of the duty can be inferred
by looking at its surrounding context within the Qur'an.[191] To
associate this word with a ritual is to relegate our reason and to
"make mockery"[192] of the Qur'an.

> O you who believe, be humble and submit, and
> worship your Lord, and do good; that you might
> prosper;
> And struggle for God with the struggle due to Him.
> He has chosen you and has not placed upon you
> hardship in the faith, the religion of your father
> Abraham; he named you as those surrendering
> before and in this, that the messenger might be a
> witness over you and that you might be witnesses
> over mankind. So set upright the duty,[193] and give
> the purity,[194] and hold fast to God. He is your Master;
> an excellent Master, and an excellent Helper.
> (22:77-78)

> We have sent down to you the Law with the truth; so
> worship God, being sincere to Him in the faith.
> Is not to God the pure faith? And those who take
> allies other than Him – "We only worship them that

---

188 Arabic transliteration added by me. Lit: they do *al-salaat.*
189 Arabic transliteration added by me. Lit: do *al-salaat.*
190 I give credit to Sam Gerrans for this translated word and refer the interested
reader to his work *The Qur'an: A Complete Revelation.*
191 I thank Sam Gerrans for this point.
192 See 31:6, 18:56.
193 I thank Sam Gerrans for this translated word.
194 I thank Sam Gerrans for this translated word.

they may bring us near to God in closeness" – God
will judge between them concerning that wherein
they differ. God does not guide he who is a liar, a
rejecter.
Had God intended to take a son, He could have chosen
from what He creates whatever He willed. Glory be
to Him! He is God, the One, the Omnipotent.

(39:2-4)

Say: "I have been commanded to worship God, being
sincere to him in the faith;
And I have been commanded to be the first of those
who surrender."
Say: "I fear, if I should disobey my Lord, the
punishment of a great Day."
Say: "God do I worship, being sincere to Him in my
faith;
So worship what you will other than Him." Say: "The
losers are those who will lose themselves and their
families on the Day of Resurrection. Is that not the
clear loss?

(39:11-15)

That Day, God will pay them in full for their true faith,
and they will know that God is the clear Truth.
(24:25)

All messengers exhorted men to worship God

Alif Lam Ra. A Law who signs are established, and
then detailed, from One Wise, Aware:
Worship none but God. "I am a warner to you from
Him and a bearer of good news.
And ask forgiveness of your Lord, then turn to Him,
and He will give you a goodly enjoyment until a
stated term, and He will give everyone possessing
grace, His grace. But if you turn away, I fear for you
the punishment of a great Day.

To God is your return; and He is powerful over everything."

(11:1-4)

And We sent Noah to his people: "I am to you a clear warner:
That you worship none but God. I fear for you the punishment of a painful Day."

(11:25-26)

And to *Ad*, their brother *Hud;* he said, "O my people, worship God! You have no god other than Him. You are but forgers.

(11:50)

And to *Thamud* their brother *Salih;* he said, "O my people, worship God! You have no god other than Him. It is He who produced you from the ground and settled you therein, so ask forgiveness of Him, then turn to Him; my Lord is near and responsive.

(11:61)

And to *Madyan* their brother *Shuaib*; he said, "O my people, worship God! You have no god other than Him. And do not decrease the measure and the balance. I see you in prosperity, but I fear for you the punishment of an encompassing Day.

(11:84)

Worship according to the Qur'an

If we study the Qur'an carefully, we do not find any specific ritual, mantra, offering or hymn that God has commanded us to perform in order to worship Him.[195] So, how are we supposed to worship God? We find the answer in the first chapter of the Qur'an.

---

195 Of course, God has given us various supplications in the Qur'an, but there is no specific hymn, ritual or prayer that must be performed religiously.

In the Name of God, the Almighty, the Merciful.
Praise belongs to God, the Lord of all Being,
The Almighty, the Merciful,
Sovereign of the Day of the faith.
It is You we worship, and You we ask for help.
Guide us to the straight path,
The path of those whom You have blessed, not of
those with whom You are angry, nor of those who
are in error.

(1:1-7)

In the verses above, the text before the word *worship* includes calling to God by invoking His name, recounting his attributes of Almightiness and Mercy, glorifying Him, testifying to His rightful status as the Lord of all Being, recounting His attributes once again and, finally, testifying to His dominion on the Day, when every soul will be rewarded for what it did. This is the essence of *worship* according to the Qur'an.

Call to God alone

When a calamity strikes, man is reminded of the truth that none can help him besides God. In that brief moment he forsakes his idols and calls to God alone.

Say: "Have you considered: if God's punishment came upon you, or the Hour came upon you, would you call to other than God, if you should speak truthfully?"
Nay, to Him you would call, and He would remove that for which you called to Him, if He willed, and you would forget those whom you make partners.

(6:40-41)

It is He who drives you in the land and the sea until, when you are in the ships, they sailing with them with a good wind, and they rejoicing therein, there comes upon them a violent wind, and the waves

come upon them from every side, and they think
that they are encompassed, they call to God, being
sincere to Him, in the faith: "If You deliver us from
this, we shall surely be among the grateful."
But when He delivers them, at once they are insolent
in the land, against right. O mankind, your insolence
is only against your souls; the enjoyment of the
lower life. Then to Us is your return, then We will
inform you of what you were doing.
(10:22-23)

Say: "My Lord commands justice. And be upright[196]
near every place of worship and call to Him, being
sincere to Him in the faith." As He originated you,
so you will return.
A faction He guided, and a faction – justified is the
error upon them; they have taken Satans as allies
other than God, and think they are guided.
(7:29-30)

So call to God, being sincere to Him in the faith,
though the rejecters dislike it.
(40:14)

He is the Living; there is no god except Him. So call
to Him, being sincere to Him in the faith. Praise
belongs to God, the Lord of all Being.
(40:65)

Say: "O mankind, if you are in doubt of my faith, I do
not worship those whom you worship other than
God, but I worship God who causes you to die, and
I am commanded that I be of the believers,"
And set upright your face to the faith, natural
monotheism, and be not of the makers of partners;

---

196 Lit: set upright your faces.

And do not call, other than God, to that which neither
  benefits you nor harms you, for if you did, then you
  will be of the wrongdoers.
And if God touches you with harm, there is no
  remover of it except Him; and if He intends good
  for you, none can repel His grace. He causes it to
  fall upon whoever He wills of His servants and He
  is the Forgiving, the Merciful.
(10:104-7)

Glorify, thank and ask forgiveness of God

And We know that your breast is straitened by what
  they say.
So glorify with the praise of your Lord, and be of the
  submitted,
And worship your Lord, until the Certain comes to
  you.

(15:97-99)

O you who believe, eat of the good things which We
  have provided you, and be grateful to God, if it is
  Him you worship.

(2:172)

So eat of what God has provided you lawful and good.
  And be grateful for the blessing of God, if it is Him
  you worship.

(16:114)

And of His signs are the night and the day, and the
  sun and the moon. Do not submit to the sun or to
  the moon, but submit to God who created them, if
  it is Him you worship.
And if they be arrogant, then those who are near their
  Lord glorify Him by night and day, and do not tire.

(41:37-38)

So submit to God and worship!
(53:62)

Say: "I am prohibited to worship those who you call on other than God when the clear signs have come to me from my Lord, and I am commanded to surrender to the Lord of all Being."
(40:66)

The futility of worshipping others

And recite to them the report of Abraham
When he said to his father and his people, "What do
   you worship?"
They said, "We worship idols, and remain devoted to
   them.
He said, "Do they hear you when you call,
Or do they benefit or harm you?"
They said, "But we found our fathers doing thus."
(26:69-74)

And it will be said to them, "Where is that you used
   to worship
Other than God? Can they help you or help
   themselves?"
(26:92-93)

Say: "I am prohibited to worship those who you call on other than God." Say: "I do not follow your desires, for I would then have erred, and would not be of the guided."
(6:56)

Do not worship Satan

The believers must call upon God alone when they are tested. The Qur'an presents an example of a man who worships

God "upon an edge."[197] As soon as God puts him in a trial, he turns towards Satan's tyranny, asking it for help.

> And among mankind is one who worships God upon
> an edge. If good befalls him, he is content with it,
> and if a trial befalls him, he turns about upon his
> face. He loses this lower life and the Hereafter; that
> is the clear loss.
> He calls to other than God that which neither harms
> him nor benefits him; that is the far error.
> He calls to him whose harm is nearer than his benefit
> – a wretched protector, and a wretched associate.
> (22:11-13)

The Qur'an makes it clear that those who make partners with God are actually in a partnership with Satan's tyranny. They pin their hopes and desires on a system which deceives them again and again.

> And the Day when He will gather them all together,
> then He will say to the angels, "Were these
> worshipping you?"
> They will say, "Glory be to You! You are our Ally,
> other than them; rather, they were worshipping the
> *elites*, most of them believed in them."
> "So today, you possess no power over each other to
> benefit or harm." And We shall say to those who
> wronged, "Taste the punishment of the Fire, which
> you used to deny."
> (34:40-42)

> "And be separated today, you criminals!"
> Did I not enjoin upon you, O Children of Adam, that
> you do not worship Satan – He is a clear enemy to
> you
> And that you worship Me? This is a straight path.

---

197 22:11.

And He has led into error a great majority of you; did
  you not understand?
(36:59-62)

Gather those who did wrong, and their companions,
  and what they were worshipping,
Other than God, and guide them to the path of the
  Fire.
But stop them, they are to be questioned:
"What is the matter with you, why do you not help
  each other?"
Rather, they are today in surrender.
And they will approach one another, questioning,
They will say, "You used to come to us from the right."
They will reply, "Rather, you were not believers;
And we had no authority over you; rather, you were a
  transgressing people.
So justified is our Lord's saying upon us, we are tasting
  it.
And we led you astray, we were ourselves astray."
(37:22-32)

And the Fire will be presented to the astray.
And it will be said to them, "Where is that you used
  to worship
Other than God? Can they help you or help
  themselves?"
So they will be hurled into it, they, and the astray,
And the army of *Iblees*, all together.
They will say, while disputing therein,
"By God, we were in clear error
When we made you equal with the Lord of all Being.
And none led us astray except the criminals;
So now we have no intercessors,
Nor a loyal friend.
If only we could return, we would be among the
  believers!"
(26:91-102)

109

* * *

Tyranny 2.0 is at the cusp of its long cherished goal: complete control over the minds of men, but its architects have made a fundamental miscalculation; they have not learned from the destruction of former tyrannies. Our erudite tyrants, despite all their worldly knowledge, remain willfully ignorant of the power of God, the Severe in retribution. He will break Tyranny 2.0 just as He has broken its predecessors, provided the believers act.

> Have you not seen how your Lord did with *Ad*,
> And *Iram*, possessors of pillars,
> The like of which had not been created in the region?
> And with *Thamud*, who carved out the rocks in the
>   valley?
> And with Pharaoh, possessor of the obelisks?
> Who transgressed in the region
> And increased therein corruption.
> So your Lord loosed upon them the whip of
>   punishment.
>
> (89:6-13)

> The revelation of the Law is from God the Almighty,
>   the Knowing,
> Forgiver of sins, Acceptor of repentance, Severe in
>   retribution, Owner of Abundance; there is no god
>   but He, and to Him is the final return.
>
> (40:2-3)

REFERENCE

Books

1984, George Orwell.
Brave New World, Aldous Huxley.
COVID-19: The Great Reset, Klaus Schwab and Thierry Malleret.
How to Avoid a Climate Disaster: The Solutions We Have and the Breakthroughs We Need, Bill Gates.
The Qur'an: A Complete Revelation, Sam Gerrans.

Websites

http://corpus.quran.com
http://cuttingthroughthematrix.com
https://reader.quranite.com
https://quranite.com
http://quranix.org

Contact

http://willyounotreason.com
contact@willyounotreason.com